Culture and Performance

Culture and Performance

The Challenge of Ethics, Politics and Feminist Theory

VIKKI BELL

Oxford • New York

English edition
First published in 2007 by
Berg
Editorial offices:
First Floor, Angel Court, 81 St Clements Street, Oxford OX4 1AW, UK
175 Fifth Avenue, New York, NY 10010, USA

Berg is the imprint of Oxford International Publishers Ltd.

Library of Congress Cataloging-in-Publication Data
Bell, Vikki, 1967-
    Culture and performance : the challenge of ethics,
politics, and feminist theory / Vikki Bell. — English ed.
        p. cm.
    Includes bibliographical references and index.
    ISBN-13: 978-1-84520-104-3 (cloth)
    ISBN-10: 1-84520-104-3 (cloth)
    ISBN-13: 978-1-84520-105-0 (pbk.)
    ISBN-10: 1-84520-105-1 (pbk.)
    1. Culture—Philosophy. 2. Performative (Philosophy)
3. Subjectivity. 4. Feminist theory. 5. Ethics. I. Title.
    HM621.B475 2007
    305.4201—dc22   2006100365

British Library Cataloguing-in-Publication Data
A catalogue record for this book is available from the British Library.

ISBN 978 1 84520 104 3 (Cloth)
        978 1 84520 105 0 (Paper)

Typeset by Avocet Typeset, Chilton, Aylesbury, Bucks
Printed in the United Kingdom by Biddles Ltd, King's Lynn.

www.bergpublishers.com

For Thomas and Charlotte

Contents

Acknowledgements

I would like to record my thanks to my wonderful colleagues at Goldsmiths College, University of London, whose work I like to think of as part of a collective project in which each has a unique part. For their suggestions and conversations in relation to the issues addressed in this book special thanks to Andrew Barry, Mariam Fraser and Monica Greco. My students at Goldsmiths, especially those on my Masters option course 'Politics and Difference' over the past few years, have been the most creative critical students one could hope for. I thank them for allowing me to learn as I teach. Likewise, my friends and colleagues, Paul Gilroy, with whom I taught the course for several years, and Alberto Toscano, who has co-taught it with me of late: my gratitude for creating precious spaces for critical thought. The organizers of various conferences and seminars allowed me to air these chapters in earlier forms: thanks to Jeffrey Alexander, Davina Cooper, Scott Lash, Celia Lury, Angela McRobbie, Thomas Osborne, Sasha Roseneil, Linda Hogan, Joanna Zylinska, and the Forum for European Philosophy. For her continued inspiration and generosity I would like to thank Judith Butler. Thanks also to Les Back, Marianne Constable, Marsha Rosengarten, Leti Volpp, Tim Bewes, Vron Ware; to Lynn Huffer who gave me some wonderful comments on the whole manuscript; and to the anonymous readers for Berg publishers. My editor Tristan Palmer patiently supported the writing of this book. Wendy McMurdo kindly gave permission to reproduce her photograph on the front cover. Thanks too to my friends, especially Sam King, Tamara Joseph and Charlotte Pomery; to Ella Kerr-McCutcheon; to my sisters, Jo and Katie, and my parents, Claire and David Bell.

Finally, my partner and children have been remarkably patient with mummy's work. Paul, thank you for all your support. Thomas and Lottie, I dedicate this book to you with all my love.

Chapter 3 extends an earlier version that appeared in *Feminist Theory* Vol 2: 2 (2001). An earlier version of Chapter 4 was published in *Economy & Society* Vol 31: 4 (2002).

Preface

This earth is anything but a sharing of humanity. It is a world that does not even manage to constitute a world; it is a world lacking in world, and lacking in the meaning of world ....

   Compassion is the contagion, the contact of being with one another in this turmoil. Compassion is not altruism, nor is it identification; it is the disturbance of violent relatedness.

Jean-Luc Nancy, *The Inoperative Community*

In a wonderful short film, director Samira Makhmalbaf offered a response to the events of September 11, 2001.[1] A young woman teaching Afghan refugees in Iran gathers her young children, encouraging them to class, remarking on the futility of the village's efforts to build a shelter in response to the USA's intention to attack Afghanistan. 'Bricks won't stop atomic bombs' the schoolteacher declares; besides, she points out, although they were Afghans, they were in Iran now. Once gathered, she questions the children, asking them what important incident had occurred in the world; hesitantly, a few venture an answer, revealing the worlds in which they live. Two people had fallen down a well, says a little boy; a little girl reports that her auntie had been buried to her neck in Afghanistan and stoned to death. These were not the answers the teacher sought and, passing over these 'local' events, she impassively tells the children that a 'global incident' had occurred that could trigger a world war and that put them in danger. 'They may drop the atomic bomb on us and we will all be killed', she says, before summarizing the incident: 'In America, in New York City, two airplanes hit the World Trade Centre towers.' She asks the children who did this, and one boy suggests 'God'. This offering sparks a conversation amongst the children on God's role in creation and destruction.

Despite the warning that a threat hangs over them, the teacher requests that the children keep silent for a minute to honour those who had died in New York. This is difficult for the young children, and they keep talking, caught up in a train of thought about why such bad things happen when it is God himself who makes people. Then why would he destroy them? 'God's not crazy enough to kill people and then remake them!' 'Does God kill?' 'God hasn't got airplanes.' 'He wants to make new people.' The teacher does not seek the trading of opinions between her young charges, however; she seeks quiet contemplation. Their chatter disallows such thoughtfulness, and with exasperation she takes them outside and has them stand beneath the soaring chimney of a local factory to attempt a minute of silence once more. 'Look at the chimney. Think of all those people in the towers who died under the rubble.' In silence, they look up, craning their necks, squinting skyward. This exposure to height, to the sheer sense of scale is intended, one infers, to convey the shock of the attack, the unexpected and horrific interruption. The children mimic the posture of those on the streets of Manhattan watching as that scene developed. Their bodies are positioned so as to experience a connection as they are implicitly invited to employ their imaginations in order to make that connection, to let it dwell within them, to allow their own bodies to take in the thought 'what if?' and to let it reverberate within. Seemingly, it is an appeal to the children to connect, if not precisely to identify, with those upon whom these acts were committed.

This film is rich in pathos, of course, but it is a pathos that operates on several levels. Explicitly, the shaming function of children is employed here. If children can attempt such connection, why can't adults? Why aren't more adults like the schoolteacher, showing the children modes of connecting, inviting forms of proximity rather than distance? If the young have at least the potential to make connections, why do we grown-ups teach them to feel and think otherwise? But the film simultaneously solicits a critique of the naivety of this line of questioning and its assumptions. First, the viewer can only suppose that the exercise is efficacious, that a connection is made, even that this is the schoolteacher's intention. Perhaps the children find the imaginative task too difficult to achieve any sense of identification. Isn't bodily mimicry so often performed for negative, non-connective, effect?[2] Perhaps the teacher does not intend such a connection? And secondly, even if the necessity of a simple empathetic humanity is the film's 'message', as viewers of the film we also know that this film does not come from the children themselves nor even their teacher. We know that this 'ethical experiment' is staged, that the response to September 11 is coming from the director's imagination.

But this critique cannot be allowed to become dismissive. The performative force of the film is not diminished by the fact that it is staged for the camera. Indeed, considering the performative force of the film involves much more than an evaluation of the success of a 'message' – the gloomy and generalized reaffirmation of the importance of educating our children for the sake of a better world – because it is a performance that performs anew at each showing. And as such the film itself is an intervention, to some extent tangential to its content. Simply put, to view this gentle, quiet film is to build a response to it in the time of its appearance. Now, some years after this film was made, one is struck by the way it provokes comment on the USA administration's response to the attack, the 'war on terror', the wars in Afghanistan and Iraq, and indeed, on the threat that presently hangs over Iran itself (as it has recently been referred to the Security Council by the United Nations' International Atomic Energy Agency in relation to its suspected ambition to develop its nuclear capabilities). And when viewed in such terms, does not the pathos shift and become centred in turn upon the naivety of the teacher who requests that the children gaze up presumably to prompt an identification of sorts with the people of New York *as if it were the latter* who required empathy? What, we might well ask, is the point of feeling empathetic with the people of New York who quite frankly, have so little exposure to images of contemporary Afghanistan or Iran, so few prompts to identification with the peoples there, so few teachers returning the exercise? It is thus to confront one's own naivety at a flickering hope as the children participate in their teacher's task. Their ability to empathize is neither here nor there on the global scene. We know this. And for these reasons, we might opine, the film performs as a comment on the connections that have *not* been made, on the compounding of violence with violence, and these facts are made all the more affecting through the connections the viewer of the short film is invited to make with the children, their teacher (and the film-makers). If one concludes 'it is *they* to whom attention should be turned, and for whom one should wish the world would be still for a minute' one also knows how little concern global events and governance have had for such ethical experiments. Moreover, we know how little change a short film is going to prompt. The film's experiment, like the teacher's, is primarily an aesthetic-contemplative exercise. To speak about this film as if it were an intervention on the geopolitical scene is laughable, if not pathetic, when the deployment of ethical imagination outside its viewing remains caught in the baldest of dichotomies, its terms of analysis unable to capture as subtle a set of emotions as how the children of Afghan refugees in Iran might feel about the turn of global events. And to reach this point is to become-child, to be caught up in an infantilizing process in which one considers oneself both naive and powerless, and renders teachers and film-makers, alike, impotent. This moment is an important one, I believe, and it is so because within its pessimism it forces a humility in relation to the fleeting nature of one's interventions; its importance is also that it obliges one to consider why one continues to observe the world, to despise its cruelties and to appreciate its creativity: why make such films? And more pertinent here, why write?

I offer this brief comment on Samira Makhmalbaf's work because it plunges one into several of the questions and concerns that preoccupy me in this book. First, it dramatizes scenes of identification in the context of geopolitics, made all the more poignant given that we the audience know what was to happen 'next'. Just as the film can be viewed as a comment on the forming, continuing, interrupting and rearranging of identifications, so this book is concerned in large part with the processes by which identities are constituted within power relations, and in particular with that body of work which has promoted an understanding of identities and indeed cultures as *performative* achievements. The children's existence within several diagrams of power catches them within complex lines – lines of the family, ethnicity, the nation, religion, those of geopolitical relations – which they are invited, and indeed obliged, to continue or at least to negotiate. How we conceptualize the invitation–obligation, however, will depend crucially upon how the power of these lines is comprehended. Since this book has as its aim the exploration of the implications of the concept of performativity, it has as its initial task an introduction to the promise of the concept in this regard. Secondly, however, the film sets one on a journey of reflexive questioning as described above, in which one struggles with the role of teachers, and, ultimately, with pedagogic forms. On the heels of the legitimate question 'What is the point of understanding the processes by which subjects are constituted unless one use that analysis in an 'ethical' sense?' comes the equally legitimate: 'What ethical intervention is possible?' By virtue of its material form and technological apparatus, cinema wears its performative intervention openly. Even with documentary, one is aware that one is watching a construct, framed and packaged for your consumption and contemplation. Academic treatises may be less obviously performative; nonetheless, they are just this. Like film, they engage the reader in processes of provocation and persuasion. With a particular relevance in relation to writings about ethics, they reach out to the reader, requiring that s/he accompany them. Barthes wrote that the writer 'must cruise the reader', in the sense that s/he must seek the reader out (1975: 4). To understand the process of writing books such as this as similar to the process of film-making in this sense, is to attempt to own (up to) the notion that one's writing is performative. That said, however, as an intervention rather than a reflection on the sociopolitical world, a book such as this is also one that is in all probability, going to be laughably impotent. Even if students may read and ponder its conclusions in a university or two, to talk up its impact on the global politics would be a form of delusion. To be persuaded by its arguments on ethics and politics is ultimately as of as much probable consequence as the children successfully identifying with the people of New York. What is desired by inviting a reader's attention, putting this book in a place akin to that of a film that in turn invites us/the child to consider the tower that is already in place of another tower? For all the talk about ethics, then, is this work another aesthetic-contemplative exercise, a substitute for 'real' action? For what its worth, I would wish to answer: not quite. For although the notion of contemplation, the notion that 'mere' thought is all that is provoked, is defensible and even somewhat attractive, especially to a reader of Hannah Arendt,[3] this conclusion also mimics the infantilizing moment described above. If possible, I would like to consider writing (and reading) as containing the promise of politico-ethical intervention with all the responsibilities that implies, but without, for reasons I will describe in this book, being able to predict or even prove its efficacy in that regard. Simultaneously, then, one would wish to retain something of the humility of the becoming-child, of the one who gazes up and out at the world, knowing in other words that this intervention is in part merely an exercise in one's own small if precious adventure of freedom.

In Chapter 1, 'The promise of performativity', the title is meant in two senses. In a straightforward sense, it means that the concept is promising as an analytic tool in the task of comprehending something of how social and political relations reproduce and how they change. Presenting a partial trajectory of the concept, this chapter explains its main tenets and its utility in formulating an understanding of the production of subjectivities within power relations. Since the ascendancy of the concept already attests as much, my role in this first chapter is somewhat redundant but for the fact that the second sense in which I suggest performativity has promise is frequently muted. That is, this book argues that performativity is not an explanatory concept so much as itself part of an intervention, and, in this context, its promise is that in making such an intervention, it will bespeak possibilities without itself becoming a moralism; in other words, that it will imagine and articulate the possibility of things being 'otherwise' while not itself becoming so enamoured of power (even such a seemingly flaccid power as that of 'explanation') as to forget to question the terms and directions of its own interventions in the socio-political world. Indeed, especially for those who like myself wish to emphasize a little of its Nietzschean lineage, to speak of promises must be slightly tongue in cheek. Nietzsche's warning that those who make promises deal in a pretence that the future of human activity is both calculable and in their sights, still resounds, as well it should. Moreover, Nietzsche would remind us that the concept of performativity cannot itself make a promise in disembodied form. The promise of performativity therefore must also be that those who utilize it reflect upon how their interventions themselves perform within a contemporary context of power relations. The political question does not come after the analytic therefore; they are entwined at the outset. Thus if the way in which one is invited or obliged to partake in the lines of power within which one emerges is always a political question, it is also necessary to consider the sense in which the attempt to comprehend the operations of power are themselves a 'cutting', an intervention that, like film editing, makes a story tell-able. This is not of course to say that this story is untrue. But it is to say that its own possibility and its framing need to be continually reconsidered.

The second chapter turns to a way of comprehending the emergence of subjectivity that has been ill-considered within the analytic frame of performativity. In 'Genealogy, Generation and Partiality', I consider how genealogical modes of understanding cultural identity have been 'cut out' of the performative frame, and with good reason. Genealogy – here in the sense of kinship ties, not in the sense of a method à la Foucault – is the foremost understanding of cultural identities against which the concept of performativity is pitted. The idea that people's actions can be understood as a continuation of their ancestry, that there is something in the blood or even in the cultural legacies of the past that weighs determinatively on present actions is precisely the idea that performativity has been mobilized to counter. The argument is not that cultural differences are performed for an audience, as in those arguments that respond to media representations that contradict what Susan Sontag terms 'cherished pieties' by dismissing them as 'staged for the camera' (2003: 10).[4] Rather the argument is that one cannot understand the actions of a person as given by their 'natures', by something essential to their bodies. On the contrary, one has to comprehend the conditions of possibility within which people emerge as subjects in their contingent contexts, which is to consider the forms of subjectivity that are available, their attractions, constraints and risks. In making this argument, however, the notion of performativity has made it difficult to consider forms of bodily attachment, tending to consider individuals somehow apart from their lines of descent. Chapter 2 considers whether this tendency – a familiar one in sociological paradigms of structure and action – can be readdressed without falling into a form of essentialism or racism. The chapter is guided by the responses to just such a question offered by Jonathon and Daniel Boyarin (1993, 1995). Its focus is on how a question about 'continuities' of cultural identity should be properly taken up within a thesis on performativity. To begin to open up such a debate the chapter draws upon the work of Emmanuel Levinas, reading his controversial early piece on Hitlerism, written in 1933, alongside his analysis of paternity in later texts, specifically *Time and the Other* and *Totality and Infinity*. From these texts, one can begin to address the complex issues at stake when one attempts to address issues of lineage in the context of a fundamentally anti-racist project. Indeed, the chapter argues that one is left with a tension between partiality and multiplicity whose negotiation is ethics itself.

The work of Levinas is also central to the arguments of Chapter 3. In this chapter I argue that, if one is persuaded by the arguments of Emmanuel Levinas, the pursuit of something called 'ethical feminism' is rendered difficult since, according to Levinas, there is a hiatus between ethics and politics in so far as politics does not flow from ethics. Indeed, politics obliges one to engage in the non-ethical, so that the ethical cannot be understood as a basis for feminist politics. I suggest that it is perhaps in the way the dangers of the non-ethical are handled that politics begins. If this is so, one can refigure the question of ethics within feminism. Ethics becomes a check on freedom and politics rather than its originary source. Along with Michel Foucault and William Connolly, I argue that ethical responses, while coming from the other, have also to be subjected to genealogical critique, so that their conditions of possibility are not naturalized. One's relation to the other is a 'violent relatedness', in Nancy's words, and acting in the face of the multiple debts and multiple complicities in which one is entangled with that other must entail the rumination on one's own possibility alongside the rumination of future compossibilities.[5]

If all modes of cultural survival take place within relations of necessary complicity with power relations (as argued in Chapter 1), the articulated desire itself – for something other than this, for something otherwise – cannot be exempted from that web. The formation and articulation of political imaginations, and even the sensation of outrage which they seemingly express, inherit or borrow their figurations, their fears and quite possibly, their desires as well;[6] this is not to say that those affects are mendacious or false, just to recognize that they arise within this present infused with past figures and ways of thinking (and hoping). The fourth chapter here considers what is arguably a little dispute between two attitudes to feminist theoretical and political endeavour. My interest in the argument here is because the terms and rhetorical figures deployed indicate certain political imaginations that have themselves broader histories. Traces of these larger histories enter into 'little' disputes because they animate and colour the fears not only of individuals but also the broader sweep of political communities and formations.

To begin to understand one's adversaries and, of course, oneself within the movements of history is to posit a doubling and self-estranging (as suggested by Deleuze, 1995) that gives onto a conversation about responsibilities and their limitations. In many ways, the final chapters here, chapters 5 and 6, constitute an extended worry about responsibility and its limitations; they consider, ultimately, the possibility of theoretical endeavours and continue Nietzsche's concern with the *value* of ethics. In Chapter 5 I develop a particular way of reassessing claims for the politics of genealogical work, by considering the 'nausea' arising from its vertiginous knowledge alongside the 'anxiety' that Latour seeks (via his 'moralists') to inject into any site of closure or decision. This conversation opens onto a consideration of how the background emptiness formed of the other, the 'unchosen' possibilities, is to be understood. The suggestion that this might be understood as potentiality leads into Chapter 6 where creativity becomes crucial to the discussion.

In Chapter 6 I seek to make sense of what has been, from my location at least, the most challenging set of questions for the notion of performativity. Beyond the litigious, the most troubling and interesting critiques of performativity range from those that emanate from the philosophical to those attentive to what one might call, with all sorts of reservations, the vital order. In Deleuze's (1988) book on Foucault, the issue of resistance to life was understood as an issue of creativity, of 'a certain vitalism' (1988: 93): 'When power becomes bio-power resistance becomes the power of life, a vital power that cannot be confined within species, environment or the paths of a particular diagram. Is not the force that comes from outside a certain idea of Life, a certain vitalism, in which Foucault's thought culminates?' (1988: 93). The attempt to attend to creativity, to the possibilities for change – which must define both ethical and political endeavours – has also, in other words, to attend to how we understand processes of creativity themselves. In focusing on how creativity has been reintroduced into the discussion, from the philosophy of Bergson, Deleuze and Guattari, and Grosz, to more recent discussions of how complexity challenges sociological concerns, the chapter argues that this work is misunderstood if it is read as simply attacking or supplanting the 'paradigm' of performativity, since for much of this work this was never its intended 'target'. Moreover, as Paul Cilliers has argued this need not be regarded as curtailing thought: 'the view from complexity claims that we cannot know complex things completely ... modest positions are inescapable ... We can increase the knowledge we have of a certain [complex] system, but this knowledge is limited ... The fact that our knowledge is limited is not a disaster, it is a condition for knowledge. Limits *enable* knowledge' (2005: 263). Its critical impact has to be felt, however, by those who have employed 'performativity'. I argue that that impact can only make theorists all the more attentive to the way we comprehend present ethical and political potentialities, reinforcing the need to consider how one's own 'cuttings' and rearrangements might take on a new sense of, or rather *as*, ethical and political invention.

One cannot hope that theoretical work can provide an adequate response to Nancy's morose list that specifies for him the situation of the earth and humans and that begins 'Bosnia-Herzegovina, Chechnya, Rwanda, Bosnian Serbs, Tutsis, Hutus, Tamil Tigers, Krajina Serbs, Casamance, Chiapas, Islamic Jihad ...' (2000: xii) and continues until he comments 'it would be difficult to bring this list to an end if the aim was to include all the places, groups or authorities that constitute the theatre of bloody conflicts among identities' (2000: xii). But one can indicate a shared desire that such a list might read as past, as fading history, in the future; if this, like the pursuit of 'feminism', means attaching oneself to 'ideals' (and even 'dreamworlds', Buck-Morss, 2000), then one needs to proceed cautiously. Since all interventions are cutting, all are properly accompanied by the risk of a reframing and deserved deflation; interventions that follow 'ideals' are especially cutting and especially 'vulnerable' in this sense. Rightly so. Arendt may well have agreed with Badiou in so far as she frequently sensed how interventions become unresponsive (and even evil) where they become guided unthinkingly by ideals. She foreshadows Badiou's (2000) concerns if only to the extent that they both recognize the potential cruelty of such a pursuit. Arendt understood, as would Badiou, as did Deleuze – who quotes Dostoevsky statement 'it was too idealistic and therefore cruel'[7] – that idealistic desire all too quickly becomes pleasure, a return to the self. I have tried not to be idealistic in this book. While I am acutely aware of the pleasures of affirmation and fidelity, I have attempted to address instead what I have found to be the most perplexing of questions in this arena of thought, since these questions are the most interesting. One has to be courageous, to assert that the circulation of these interventions has a potential value, while at the same time, one has to maintain the humility of which I spoke above, and understand that that assertion must simultaneously invite a reframing in which the ideals as well as the details and processes are legitimately interrogated. Although I have not tried to be 'good', I have tried to be interesting, trusting that if I fail in that, forgiveness is only secondarily a divine quality.[8]

Vikki Bell
London

CHAPTER 1

The Promise of Performativity:
Theory and/as Political Ethic

But how could I deny that I possess these hands and this body, and withal escape being classed with persons in a state of insanity, whose brains are so disordered and clouded by dark bilious vapours as to cause them pertinaciously to assert that they are monarchs when they are in the greatest poverty; or clothed [in gold] and purple when destitute of any covering; or that their head is made of clay, their body of glass, or that they are gourds?

Descartes, Meditations 1

Performativity as Coextensivity: 'No Interiority'

'Performativity' could no doubt be given various introductions and genealogies. Here, understood as a development within a much wider movement against Descartes' *cogito*, the notion of performativity names an approach that refuses to tie the fact that 'there is thinking' to identity or ontology. In place of the certainty that I am – the *cogito* – is an argument for *coextensivity*. Contra Descartes, 'thinking' is only confirmation that an individual exists within a discursive world; no certainty arises from the fact of thinking. Rather, the state of doubt from which Descartes began his *Meditations* continues, since 'the subject', in this rendering, is understood as coextensive with his or her outside. There is no resolution of doubt, no passage into certainty, because the subject is itself the locus of effects of his or her surroundings. That is, the subject is produced by historically varying conditions that are in turn sustained by their produced elements.

Understood in a shorter trajectory from Nietzsche's fiery 'there is no doer behind the deed' via Foucault's use of the Panopticon by which he sought to present the exercise of productive power/knowledge relations diagramatically, to Judith Butler's feminist rendering of the argument, this coextensivity is a radical critique of any originary notion of interiority. Any presumption of a subject at work 'behind' the action is precisely that: a presumption. And any sense of an interiority – what Butler calls the 'trope' of interiority – into which the subject him or herself can 'look' and thereby enact a conscience, a subjectivity, is an *effect*, it is argued, of the configurations in which the subject is 'caught'. Because these configurations are configurations of power, the tracing of their productivity is, in the hands of these authors, always understood as a matter of analysing power-effects. In this trajectory, therefore, the term 'performativity' emerges to name an argument with a certain history of political critique. Thus, while the term itself comes from the study of linguistics, was coined by J. L. Austin (1962) and further elaborated by Searle's *Speech Acts* (1969), its adoption within feminist and sociocultural analyses imported it into this trajectory, where its implications have meant that the term developed far beyond a theory of language. In this first section I will trace this trajectory to illustrate the sense in which the concept 'performativity' entails more than a focus on language. Its meaning has become thoroughly attached to a series of arguments about the constitution of interiority that were always concerned with the analysis of contemporary power relations and, as a corollary, with the constitutive nature of ethical judgements.

In Nietzsche's *Genealogy of Morality*, the argument that 'the deed is everything' (1967/1887: 45) arises within the context of his critique of the man of *ressentiment*, the figure of the Christian who interprets his own weakness as freedom, as willed, as a meritorious deed. The notion of 'the subject' (or the soul, 1967/1887: 45) is 'a fiction added to the deed', a fiction that also erroneously 'separates the lightening from its flash and takes the latter for an *action*, for the operation of a subject called lightening'. (1967/1887: 45). This belief, which in fact 'doubles the deed; it posits the same event as cause and then a second time as its effect', underpins a way of thinking about morality that justifies inaction and mediocrity. It affords a sense of 'us, the good' to those who in fact do nothing other than hide away, avoiding evil and desiring little from life, leaving revenge up to God and exhibiting a 'prudence of the lowest order' (1967/1887: 46). These men of *ressentiment* alternately gasp and sneer at those to whom they give the appellation 'evil', and against whom they define themselves positively. Nietzsche's contention is not that the targets of *ressentiment* are morally superior, but he did want to argue that they do at least *act* whereas the man of *ressentiment*'s action is only ever *reaction*. Nietzsche's argument that there is no doer behind the deed is part of an argument therefore that (Christian) morality can be used to judge well those who do little but judge others negatively. Furthermore, this morality that redefines a reactionary and weak stance as 'good', Nietzsche contends, that masquerades as a love of justice and egalitarianism, turns in fact on a less abstract desire for retaliation, for revenge: it is in fact a desire for strength. The man of *ressentiment* hates 'the strong', but wants to become them, to be able to act as they act.

For Nietzsche, therefore, the argument that there is 'no doer behind the deed' is made in the context of an argument that the strong cannot and should not be asked to refrain from strength, as if the subject were separate from his strength, free to exercise it or not. It is those suggesting such restraint who are the target of his attack in so far as they perpetuate a mediocrity by attempting to rein in those whose action at least potentially might allow human brilliance to develop.

Moreover, Nietzsche's critique of morality extends to an analysis of the notion of 'bad conscience', which is precisely for him an attempt to 'socialize' human nature, to turn man's instincts of freedom inward. The inner world expands, as it were, gaining 'depth, breadth and height' as the political organization of morality installed something called 'bad conscience'. Seemingly stemming from within, this bad conscience is developed as new regimes declare war on the instincts that had hitherto given humankind its strength and its joy as well as its 'terribleness' (1967/1887: 85). The sense of an interiority to which I referred above emerges from this process in which man is turned against himself – the 'internalization' of man. His 'soul', that is, his internalization of morality, that which would henceforth require constant vigilance and self-monitoring, resulted from what Nietzsche calls an act of violence. Indeed, it results from the founding act of 'the state' that attempts to give form to the formless populace (1967/1887: 86) and that thereby requires the perpetuation of such violence.

Nietzsche's arguments are provocative not least because, in so far as they express his admiration for strength and human brilliance, they clash with modern sensibilities, as of course they would (since his point is their critique). Indeed, his arguments are provocative despite – there again, perhaps because of – their potential to cause offence; they insist that one's suspicions should be aroused by any mode of moral criticism that implies a superiority on the part of the one who judges. For present purposes, I mean to emphasize how his arguments about the constitution of an interiority with which the subject himself wrestles, with which he spends time, monitoring and questioning himself, is not merely his description of how one comes to have a conscience or soul, nor what it means to have a conscience or a soul, but must be read as part of his wider ranging critique of morality and those who preach morality to others based on an image of themselves as the righteous. The doubting of interiority, of 'identity', is simultaneously a doubting of ethical judgement. Nietzsche's work suggests any investigation of the political conditions under which morality is constituted fails where it itself becomes a form of moralism.

In his *Discipline and Punish*, Foucault was of course indebted to Nietzsche, as he clearly alludes in the opening chapter. Foucault suggests that his study is an attempt to consider the 'entry of the soul on to the scene of penal justice' by considering it, and the corpus of scientific knowledge surrounding it, as an effect of power relations (1975: 24). Where Nietzsche described how pleasure arising from punishment – 'the exalted sensation of being allowed to despise and mistreat someone as "beneath him"' (1967/1887: 65) – had been masked by notions of 'justice', Foucault pursues the way criminal justice comes to justify itself by 'perpetual reference to something other than itself, by this unceasing re-inscription in non-juridical systems' (1975: 22). Rather than a narrative of progress towards leniency, Foucault wanted to argue that there has been a shift in power relations as judicial power has gradually been replaced with disciplinary forms of power. Where formerly there was the punishment, even the elimination, of the body, one is now confronted with a whole apparatus whose aims are rather different. With the rise of disciplinary power relations, bodies are attended to as replete with potential and are invested with capabilities. Without rehearsing all aspects of Foucault's well-known argument, it is important to emphasize how, in certain specific senses, disciplinary power does not simply train bodies to comply with its regimes so that resistance is quelled, but produces forms of embodiment that actively partake in their own subjection: disciplinary power *invests* the body in a way that earlier regimes of punishment did not.

There is a training of the body, which from the point of view of power is a 'rendering docile'; yet whereas previously a body's inaction indicated the workings of power, now it is the bodies' actions that signal power's success. Not only are the bodies Foucault describes in *Discipline and Punish* (1975) the collective recipients of disciplinary regimes – required to follow timetables that coordinate each of them collectively in space and time, for example, their eating, sleeping, praying, exercise, reading and so on – but they must also undertake an individual training that will coordinate each limb, each glance, each gesture. In this sense the disciplined body is one that having received the attentions of power, comes to embody its trace in the smallest detail. Thus the schoolboy bespeaks power in the placement of his feet, the extension of his spine, the grip of his pencil, the formation of his letters. The training becomes habit, initially responding then sustaining these attentions of power. Power is sustained, moreover, without passing through consciousness. As Foucault describes, the lines of force are taken in, concealed as they are enfolded. 'In all his work,' wrote Deleuze, 'Foucault seems haunted by this theme of an inside which is merely the fold of the outside, as if the ship were a folding of the sea' (Deleuze, 1988: 97).

For Foucault, the operations of disciplinary power become the conditions of possibility for a scientific knowledge about the population there constituted. By gathering bodies within disciplinary regimes, by attended to them as individual bodies, by monitoring, recording and measuring them as individual 'cases' there could simultaneously arise a knowledge of them as a group, a scientific knowledge that could begin to speak about norms and exceptions. This knowledge 'compares, differentiates, hierarchizes, homogenizes, excludes. In short, it normalizes' (1975: 183). Through their objectification, therefore, a 'corpus of scientific knowledge' was made possible. And as these knowledges – such as psychiatry, psychology, pedagogy, criminology 'and so many other strange sciences' (1975: 226) – develop, so their experts come to take their role within penal systems and elsewhere (such as in hospitals, in schools, and beyond the institutions in society more generally), commenting on the case before them in relation to a body of knowledge built upon the objectification of his or her 'population'. In this way, the relations between power and knowledge are perpetuated.

The subjects of this knowledge come to partake in the operations of power themselves, complying with it even as they emerge and assert themselves as skilled bodies and active subjects. This normalizing power objectifies bodies, then, and subjects them to the attentions of power; but it simultaneously makes subjects *of* them as they begin not only to act but also to think and speak (of) themselves as discipline and its knowledges organize them so to do. A relationship of self to self is instituted as the subject is obliged to look 'inward' as looking 'up' yields less and less insight, folding whatever desire prompted such a gaze back on itself. In other words, the attentions of disciplinary power open up an *interiority* as the subject ponders, compares, measures and chastises herself against prevailing abstract norms, be they social, scientific, moral or developmental. In this, the argument elaborates Nietzsche on the development of bad conscience. The prisoner in the cell of the Panopticon, for example, ponders his crime and considers the error of his ways, thereby opening up a 'space' for something he calls (moral) conscience. The schoolchild considers his or her performance and opens up a 'space' for something called intelligence. For the hospital patient, this interiority is termed 'health', and so on. Each disciplinary regime produces a notion that appears to call for the regime's regulation but which in truth owes its very conditions of possibility to the operations of power.

The folding of power into the body is therefore, and simultaneously, an objectification and a subjectification. In Deleuze's explanation: 'a line of subjectification is a process, a production of subjectivity in a social apparatus [*dispositif*]: it has to be made, inasmuch as the apparatus allows it to come into being or makes it possible' (1992: 161). Here then is Foucault's infamous circularity, for the rise of new forms of objectification brought with them new forms of subjectification, as the processes of normalization meant not only that individuals were compared but, as disciplinary power takes hold, were to compare themselves with a scientifically produced figure of the 'normal'. Subjects consequently arise who are individuated but without individuality (Han, 1998: 122); or whose individuality is only understood as such in relation to a norm against which they are compared. Such a mode of subjectification serves to bind them tighter still within the disciplinary power/knowledge relations.

Because the possibility of human sciences, and indeed the very possibility of 'man', is intimately related to the political subjection of bodies in this way, any knowledges which appear to look deep into his constitution have to be placed under scrutiny. This argument was of course developed in Foucault's next work – the history of sexuality – which can be read as an extended genealogy of psychoanalysis, an investigation into its conditions of possibility, since the argument of that book is that the deployment of sexuality created the foundational notion of 'sex' in just the way that 'man' appears to tether the human sciences. As Foucault asks: 'Is 'sex' really the anchorage point that supports the manifestations of sexuality, or is it not rather a complex idea that was formed inside the deployment of sexuality? In any case, one could show how this idea of sex took form in the different strategies of power and the definite role it played therein' (Foucault, 1981: 152). The notion of sex – like the notion of the soul – is deployed and sustained within power relations that ground their *raison d'être* in its givenness while disguising the petty, routine, but systematic technologies and practices that circle a void.

If the inside – what is commonly believed to be 'expressed' in the subject's words and actions – has no genuine interiority but is produced coextensively with its outside, if we remain Nietzschean to the extent that we concede we are necessarily 'strangers to ourselves' (1967/1887: 15), then the subject has always to be approached as an element within a wider schema that produces and constrains how it is possible to emerge as a subject. Thus Foucault's interest was always, he remarked in an interview, in 'how the human subject fits into games of truth, whether they were truth games that take the form of a science or refer to a scientific model, or truth games such as those one might encounter in institutions or practices of control' (1994/1984: 281). The process of producing oneself as a subject is a response to the truths that are sustained by the power relations within which one moves; even one's deepest and most intimate comprehensions of self reflect their exterior constitutive forces. As Judith Butler puts it in her *Undoing Gender*: 'I am outside myself from the outset, and must be, in order to survive, and in order to enter into the realm of the possible' (2004a: 32).

Via Butler's work, the concept of performativity has become a tool of analysis by which to interrogate differentiated subject formation within practices that sustain lines of power and power-effects. Butler took the term from the study of linguistics and tied it to the critical tradition discussed above. A performative utterance, for Austin, was one in which 'the issuing of the utterance is the performing of an action' (2004/1962: 163), such that the saying of the utterance – his classic examples were 'I do (take this woman to be my lawful wedded wife) and 'I name this ship the *Queen Elizabeth*' – is not to describe my doing but 'to do it': 'When I say, before the registrar or altar, &c., "I do", I am not reporting on a marriage: I am indulging in it' (2004/1962: 163). These utterances are often taken, mistakenly in his view, to be the outward description, true or false, of 'the occurrence of the inward performance' (2004/1962: 164), sometimes understood as a spiritual inward performance. It is his challenge to the idea that there needs be an inward act to accompany these performative utterances that foreshadows Butler's use of his thesis. For while Austin's ultimate concern was to explicate the requisite conditions for the smooth or 'happy' functioning of a performative, it is crucial to his argument that performatives – even the 'awe-inspiring' 'I promise to ...' (2004/1962: 164) – cannot be considered within the terms of truth and falsehood. Even one who promises in bad faith, still, in uttering the words, makes the promise. A promise has been made; something has been done, and something is set in motion.

It is the insistence upon the non-necessity of an 'inward' performance to accompany the 'outer' performative that enables Austin's thesis to be tied to the tradition of critical thought indicated above. In her text *Gender Trouble* Butler argued that the gendered subject is an outward performance sustained without the necessity of any prior or contemporaneous 'inward act'. The idea that there is such an interiority – one that 'causes' the subject's gender or that his or her actions 'express' – is the cultural fiction that 'discrete and polar genders' flow from the seeming duality of anatomical sex (1990: 140). The notion that there are two discrete genders is a fabrication, a performative achievement that is sustained through the production and repetition of 'corporeal signs' (1990: 136). Butler's own summary of *Gender Trouble* in her later book *The Psychic Life of Power* may be useful here: 'the performance of gender retroactively produces the effect of some true and abiding feminine essence or disposition, so that one cannot use an expressive model for thinking about gender. Moreover I argued that gender is produced by ritualised repetition of conventions, and that this ritual is socially compelled in part by the force of a compulsory heterosexuality' (1997b: 144). Gendered bodies do not express gender difference, in other words, but – to use Austin's resonant phrase – *indulge* in it; gender must be seen as a continuing series of actions, behaviours, gestures that occur in relation to conditions of the present, not a propelling force emanating from within the body. This 'indulgence', therefore, is a series of actions performed under conditions of compulsion, constrained by the particular assemblage of power/knowledge relations within which it takes place. Attention must be given therefore to how the subject's embodiment is produced, how it literally incorporates the lines of force and knowledge that surround it in a process that is ongoing. To consider the process of subjectification one has therefore to attend to the diagrams of power and enunciation within which the subject is incorporated and that sustain the subject as it simultaneously both indicates and sustains these wider matrices of power and knowledge.

Just as Foucault's work can be understood as a genealogy of psychoanalysis, and hence as an argument that even the most intimate expressions of self, for example, in sexual desire, must be understood within the complex of power/knowledge relations that he terms the deployment of sexuality, so too Butler's work has insisted that the subject's viability is, if you like, a *cultural* question. If the bland and amorphous term 'culture' does too much work and too little to illuminate here, it does at least convey something of the idea that how a subject is produced and sustained relates to the specificity of its environment as well as the sense in which subjects always emerge as part of wider shared processes. But in so far as the task is to emphasize the relationship between lines of force and the process by which the body is obliged to signal its participation as a matter of survival, the term culture needs fortification.[1]

The term 'culture' or 'cultural' needs to be heard as an invocation of an analysis that has issues of political critique at its heart. This is arguably what the critique of Butler that circled around the term 'cultural' somehow 'forgot' (Fraser, 1997; Butler, 1997c), as culture became reduced to recognition and relegated to an immaterial relation. Indeed, as the theoretical trajectory that has been briefly mapped out here indicates, this work continues a history of such critique.

For this reason, better than 'cultural' alone, the term 'cultural survival' serves to illuminate Butler's central thesis (Butler, 1990: 139; see also Bell, 1999a). This term goes some way to insisting that 'performativity' must be analysed alongside political relations, and we will return to it below. For Butler argues that to attempt to exist outside contemporary norms or terms of intelligibility is not impossible but it is to risk incomprehension and even sanction, to the extent that there will be those who will not allow such contraventions or who will regard the attempt as in itself a provocation to violence.[2] Conversely, to partake in the cultural fiction of gender is to secure one's own 'cultural survival' in a world where genders are distinct, hierarchically related and heteronormatively organized. This thesis is not merely about presenting oneself as a gendered being within the heterosexist matrix, therefore, but is about the very process of coming into being. In *Bodies that Matter*, Butler wrote:

> The process of that sedimentation or what we might call materialisation will be a kind of citationality, the *acquisition of being* through the citing of power, a citing that establishes an originary *complicity with power* in the formation of the 'I'. (1993: 15)

While each citation is 'anew', therefore, it is always constrained in advance by the power/knowledge relations that arrange both the conditions of possibility – and in that sense 'precede' without being causal in relation to the performance (since they are only ever sustained through the performance[3]) – and the structures of intelligibility that surround that citation (see Butler, 1997a: 127–63). The subject has to engage with structures that are disciplinary for its very survival. The subject emerges through that engagement.

But *Gender Trouble* was not a programmatic work; its more limited ambition was to trouble the categories of gender as they then circulated. The thesis was an elaboration of theoretical work, but it also pointed to contemporary prac-tices– such as drag – in order to ask what these practices said about the 'norms' at stake. Thus the categories of 'butch' and 'femme' raise the question, are these copies of original, heterosexual gender roles? To which Butler answered: there is no original. Butler recalls that her argument was that 'categories like butch and femme were not copies of a more originary heterosexuality, but they showed how the so-called originals, men and women within the heterosexual frame, are similarly constructed, *performatively* established' (2004a: 209). To try to understand the 'copy' with reference to an 'original' is to miss the point. In other words the original is 'as performative as the copy' (2004a: 209). Men and women in the heterosexual matrix have to engage in repeated performance in relation to the norms by which that arrangement is upheld, and in doing so, engage simultaneously in a series of foreclosures that prevent its dissolution. Queer theory set itself the task of illustrating how the lines of these foreclosures are conventions, how their dictates are merely possibilities, how sexual identi-ties, practices and bodies are mobile, and do not always line up according to dominant understanding. If some performative accomplishments succeed in establishing themselves as natural, in other words, it is by 'occluding the ways in which they are performatively established' (2004a: 209).

Thus the political and ethical questions at stake have always been the primary issues for Butler. Her task is to demonstrate the foreclosures of a variety of regimes of different orders. The point is not to prove an intellectual argument that everything is 'socially constructed'; rather it is to investigate these specific foreclosures or exclusions that constrain the possibilities of the subject even as they enable that subject to emerge (see also Nealon, 1998). This is the paradox that surrounds the emergent subject: specific sets of cul-tural and political norms and relations proffer the subject his or her opportu-nity to become, to emerge, while binding her to them for her intelligibility.

Butler's questions concern how to articulate a response to those regimes while remaining cognizant of the contradictions in positing an escape, an 'un-disciplined' route to a place beyond these regimes. Foreclosures are not akin to decisions such that one might refuse, reverse or alter them; that something, some route of being or becoming is foreclosed means that it does not even arise as a possibility. Culturally, and thus psychically, it is foreclosed. The 'how to' question is not so much for the emergent subject, therefore, although that it certainly is, but for the cultural critic herself. That is, the analysis of the fragility of cultural survival, what it entails politically and ethically for the subject, has always to be coupled with Nietzsche's corrective. The analysis of the processes by which a notion of interiority is established, in other words, has always to be coupled with a questioning of one's own values, with a genealogy thereof. Such a question is not to revert to a focus on the self. Quite the opposite: one must question one's own values precisely because one's own judgements and affinities do not escape the analyses of power/knowledge relations under scrutiny. To question one's own values, one's own potentials for judgement and moralism, is to understand one's constitution within these relations. The response need not take the form of a retreat to the self, and should not do so, since the point is precisely that the lack of interiority obliges an attention to coextensivity and thus to one's *coexistence*: existing within power, within certain temporal and spatial coordinates, within certain ways of speaking and knowing, is also a coexisting with others.

Thus the intellectual trajectory discussed in this section[4] has sought to focus attention on the key argument of coextensivity, whereby any interiority is to be comprehended in relation the arrangements of its lines of power, knowledge and subjectification (Deleuze, 1992). But it has also sought to illustrate that the analysis of 'performativity' is more than the description of these lines. The analysis is also mobilized by the need to foster a critical awareness that amounts to a political ethic. The political ethic it implies is one that comprehends the plurality implicit in the concept of performativity. This, I submit, is the promise of performativity. It is what 'performativity' sets in motion, its own performative.

From Coextensivity via Co-originality to Responsibility: Performativity and Political Ethics

In her recent work Judith Butler has made the relationship between 'performativity' and political ethics explicit. Both *Precarious Life* (2004b) and *Undoing Gender* (2004a) take up the task of showing how the fact that 'I am outside myself from the start' has profound ethical and political implications. There is, however, a middle step in the argument which is worth pursuing briefly, and which concerns what Jean-Luc Nancy calls 'co-originality'. Here 'co-originality' refers precisely to that plurality on which any origin story of the self turns, since origin cannot be represented except in such a way (Nancy, 2005).

In parts, *Precarious Life* (2004b) draws upon the figure of the child in making its argument about the relation between mourning and political ethics, a manoeuvre that Butler had employed in her earlier work *The Psychic Life of Power* (1997b). In the earlier work, she elaborates on Foucault: 'Foucault's reformulation of subordination as that which is not only pressed on a subject but forms a subject, that is, is pressed on a subject by its formation, suggests an ambivalence at the site where the subject emerges' (1997b: 6–7). Butler relates this ambivalence, this simultaneous domination and formation of the subject, to the figure of the child; she argues that Foucault's account resonates with psychoanalytic accounts in so far as it implies the passionate attachment of the subject to the power which forms her. In psychoanalysis 'no subject emerges without a passionate attachment to those on whom he or she is fundamentally dependent (even if that passion is "negative" in the psychoanalytic sense)' (1997b: 7). Because becoming a subject for Foucault entails submission, or rather – since this process does not happen once and for all – because becoming a subject requires *several* modes of submission (in different regimes, or different domains of life) by which the subject's becoming is also sustained, the emerging subject is engaged in a repeated and multi-sited attaching of itself to power. The emerging subject is dependent upon these attachments. S/he is dependent upon them in order to survive, driven only by the 'pervasively exploitable ... desire to survive, "to be"' (1997b: 7). Referencing Nietzsche, Butler argues that '[t]he child does not know to what he/she attaches; yet the infant as well as the child must attach in order to persist in and as itself' (1997b: 8). There is no choice involved, in other words, since, if one wishes to survive, one has to produce oneself through a relation with others, those proximate and those with whom the infant/child is, by definition at this stage of life, in a power relationship.

Butler insists that the emergent subject must not 'see' these attachments, for to become fully cognizant of one's formation in dependency is to lose precisely one's sense of separateness, one's 'self'. Just as children grow up to lose their fascination with their primary care-givers, even to suffer a feeling of humiliation at having loved *that* person(s), so 'the subject' must deny its dependencies in order to assert itself as a subject. Note that this subject is *continually* produced, so that the child is only a figure to introduce an argument, a less controversial way to suggest the ambivalence of subject constitution repeated throughout life. The power relations are both productive and denied: 'The "I" emerges upon the condition that it deny its formation in dependency, the conditions of its own possibility,' writes Butler (1997b: 9–10). One cannot see one's own conditions of emergence, for to be continually aware of the power relations constituting and sustaining the conditions of one's own becoming would be to exist within a kind of psychotic state. When Descartes enters a proximity with those 'madmen' who doubt their own bodies, asking 'how can I doubt these hands are mine?' he alludes precisely to this relation between not fully owning oneself and a kind of madness.[5] And it is precisely the irrationality of thinking these hands are not mine that Jean-Luc Nancy questions – why not believe it? – and that I will explore in a different way in Chapter 2. Here, the necessary denial means the subject is constantly threatened with disruption (and may even, Butler suggests, neurotically repeat primary scenes that it cannot see) (1997b: 10). The subject, therefore, with its potential to 'act' *as if* wilfully, eclipses the conditions of its inauguration that bind it to contexts and persons from whom it must continually dissociate itself in order to attain a status as a subject.

'Being-with', as Jean-Luc Nancy has written, 'is Being's own-most problem'
(2000: 30).

It is precisely this being-with, constituted by, with and *over* (these relations
to) others, that lends *Precarious Life* its focus. The child is evoked again as a
recap of the argument:

> as infants and young children, they loved their parents or other primary others in
> absolute and uncritical ways – and that something of that pattern lives on in their adult
> relationships. I may wish to reconstitute my 'self' as if it were there all along, a tacit
> ego with acumen from the start; but to do so would be to deny the various forms of
> rapture and subjection that formed the condition of my emergence as an individuated
> being and that continue to haunt my adult sense of self with whatever anxiety and
> longing I may now feel. Individuation is an accomplishment, not a presupposition, and
> certainly no guarantee. (2004: 26–7)

To understand subjectivity as constituted thus becomes a profoundly and
explicitly political question for Butler, as it was for Nietzsche and Foucault.
No subject can come into being without this relation to plurality. One emerges
through that plurality which is also a power relation such that our attachments
to power qualify the sense in which we might speak of the autonomy of the
willing subject. And not because they *limit* our capacities to act, but because
our capacities to act are moulded via these relations. Not least, subjects are
attached to power because the interiorities – the desires and motivations that
seem to characterize one's very individuality – arise through participation in
power relations. In this way, Butler wishes to emphasize, we are constituted in
relation to others, intimately related to lives that are not our own. That intimacy is not always a loving parental relationship; indeed, the physical necessity of the relation means the child is required to attach itself and experiences
the vulnerability of existing, for good or for ill, at another's hands. In her own
'anti-Oedipus' movement, Butler evokes the figure of the child therefore not
in order to reduce relationality to the Oedipal triangle, but in order to make
an argument about the subject's fundamental constitution in *plurality* such
that a sense of individuality is never an individual achievement but a relational
one, both precarious and vulnerable as a result.

Butler is writing in the context of a work that addresses the response of the
US administration to the attacks of September 11, 2001. Indeed, her discussion of the fundamental relation of the subjects to others is an exploration of
the potential for a sense of communality to arise from experiences of grieving.
In grief, she suggests, one suffers an intensely personal experience of loss; yet
we also understand through that experience that our capacity to be 'undone'
is due precisely to the fact that we require and rely upon others for our personal existence, because we fold that relation into our very sense of 'identity'.
We become ourselves through these relations. But, as the disorientation and

devastation that grief can cause illuminates, the self that one becomes is always in process, and subjectification always in a sense 'fails' because individuation can and does falter. If the relations that have had to be denied emerge to floor us, the competent and useful subject unravels a little.

Again, this argument is a slightly different take on an argument that Butler had made in earlier work, both in *Bodies that Matter* and *The Psychic Life of Power*. There, Butler had argued that melancholia might act as a sort of metaphor for performative constitution. Speaking of gender as constituted within the heterosexual frame, Butler argued that in a sense the contemporary production of sexual orientation with its related constitution of gender might be regarded as melancholic. For Freud, melancholic loss is a loss that cannot be grieved, or that cannot be 'let go' by the subject, such that the lost object is incorporated into the ego, and becomes a part of the person, constitutive of who she or he is. In Butler's hands, the production of gender can be related to this melancholia. For here, too, there is something that has been placed on the 'interior' – with the proviso that one remembers it is not truly interior – that has to be carried although (and because) it is in tension with the performance. In *Gender Trouble* Butler had argued that in the production of the heterosexual subject, there is necessarily a loss of the opportunity to be otherwise – the possibility of love, or of certain forms of love, is occluded (1990: 24) – and not just some one or some sets of people; this is about the constitution of one's subjectivity. In Butler, the psychic and the Foucauldian moments are brought together; indeed, Butler borrows from Freud the notion that there is a process of encrypting – a carrying of the tabooed love. In *The Psychic Life of Power* it is also a tabooed love, the incestuous love, that is an 'unfinishable grieving' for that which founds the subject (and that which must be continually denied for cultural survival) (see also *Undoing Gender*, 2004c). Butler argues it is 'an attachment to prohibition, an attachment which takes the form of a turning back upon itself' (1997b: 68).

To return to *Precarious Life:* in mourning, therefore, disorientation reveals an indebtedness that Butler wishes to understand as a sort of exposure. First and foremost, this exposure is to one's own vulnerability with an accompanying sense of incomprehension. For Butler, this incomprehension is 'the unconscious imprint of my primary sociality'. This is precisely Nancy's 'being-with'. Nancy would interpret the incomprehension as an exposure that is also an ex-position, a movement out of the 'self-positioning' of the subject. It is not the case, therefore, that in grief the primary and continual constitution of one's own self through plurality becomes suddenly clear, as if one suddenly had insight into the *dispositifs* that produce one's subjectivity, an insight into one's own ignorance. Rather, the argument is that one experiences something of the precarious nature of the ties – as well as perhaps of the foreclosures – that sustain one's subjectivity. In this experience of exposure one is exposed to one's dependencies and to one's own 'unknowingness'. We become strange to ourselves, exposed and ex-posed. The question is whether this experience, registered at the level of sensation, be it a sudden or creeping sensation of exposure, might in its unravelling of the subject's constitution, open up the possibility for new linkages, new constitutions? If one is exposed to our 'unknowing', born itself of an originary plurality, might a possibility for a political ethic arise, and with it, as Butler would indeed contend, the possibility of a reorientation of politics?

In her affirmation of just such a logic, Butler's political argument is one that is thoroughly micro-political in the Foucauldian (and Deleuzean) sense. Finding in the most intimate experiences an opening out onto the interrelatedness of one's very subjectivity, Butler revisits Foucault's question of one's complicities, attractions and dalliances with chimerical sources of power. Even as Butler turns her critical attention to the US administration's reactions to September 11, therefore, it is not because the state is ultimately the source of power, or the only site for the constitution of subjectivity, but because it is where there is a present danger of complicity with the sense of subjectivity there proffered. There is a responsibility to challenge the state's implicit constitution of the grieving US subject as requiring aggressive and restrictive responses. In this, the state attempts to 'capture' the sense of being undone, to put order on it in a particular way. Butler's question is whether the events might not have led – and might not still lead – in a different political direction. If the vulnerability and exposure of grief opens one out onto one's interrelations with others, if it highlights the sense of self as constituted through the 'enigmatic traces of others' (2004b: 46), might not this feeling of exposure lead one to comprehend one's self as multiply connected and indebted? Might there be a reorientation that reorders the self not by fortification but by and through the unfurling of her constitution? Revealed as precisely *co*-extensive, as *co*-originary and therefore as implicated in multiple extensions, the subject's inter-ests take it beyond its temporal and spatial locale. By pursuing the extensive nature of the subject, might not one come to regard one's most intense and in that sense proximate – genealogically or territorially proximate – attachments as themselves the rationale for broader sets of connections. Without passing through God, therefore, one might regard oneself as produced through and *over* a relationality that can arise again to reconstitute oneself differently. No higher Being is required to make this argument. The fact of plurality, of being-with, needn't imply an absolute alterity as it does for Levinas. The enigmatic traces of others to which Butler refers are only that, not the traces of God. Indeed, it is the traces of others in and as the most intimate constitutions of selfhood that, contra Levinas, might potentially open one up and out.[6]

The political ethic described in *Precarious Life* attempts to prompt new articulations of subjectivity, to challenge the coupling of mourning to an aggressive patriotism and to promote in its place what might be termed an ethic of originary plurality. Such an ethic entails an awareness of both radical complicities and radical indebtedness such that, in turn, the tasks of comprehension and of response demand attention to (in this case, global) interdependencies.

This attempt to articulate the promise, the political ethic, which accompanies the concept of performativity is, therefore, an attempt to oppose those who regard its political attitude as resigned pessimism. It is an attempt to argue that the mantra 'no interiority' need not led to a resigned political stance wherein the willing subject is understood as simply an illusion that masks the forces of power that have constituted the subject and wherein all attempts to challenge lines of power are thwarted from the outset. For the 'pessimistic' account of the subject as a trained and disciplined body in Foucault's sense, or as constituted under conditions of duress and made possible only through its attachment to power, in Butler's sense, contains also the possibility of new entanglements of power, ones that do not escape power relations but that institute new arrangements of the lines of the *dispositif*. While theorists remain necessarily guarded about delineating the possibilities of new entanglements, since they contain no guarantees, the political ethic of this work is about promoting such new arrangements, whether this remains implicit or is stated explicitly, whether it is achieved by imagining other possibilities through attention to current arrangements, or of noticing their nascent forms.

Performative Possibilities

To consider one fascinating example: Judith Hamera (2005) tells the story of a couple – Ben and May Sem – from Cambodia, Khmer survivors living in Los Angeles, who were trained in classic Khmer dance. Through their performance of this highly stylized dance form, Hamera argues, Ben and May perform an embodied 'answer' to past trauma. Their interviews with Hamera convey a sense in which their skill in embodying this 'ur-text' of Khmer culture (2005: 97) allows that culture to survive in a new setting where its meaning is altered and multiple. That is, one might argue that the training of the body results in the literal incorporation of power in Foucault's sense (a conservative process rendering the body docile, making it conform and constituting the dancer as an 'individual without individuality' as discussed above). However, seen in the wider context of the Sems' movement away from the atrocities committed by the Khmer Rouge regime,[7] this incorporation is clearly a mode and sign of survival, both theirs and the practices that constitute Khmer 'culture'. May Sem says, 'I hear my teachers who did not get out. I hear them sometimes in the day. I don't see, just hear. I am scared but they tell me the steps [movements generally] to the dance. I am like a child, a baby. I listen to them tell me the step. At first I am so scared, I don't listen. Maybe go crazy like my neighbour I tell you. But I listen to them tell me the step, then I do. I do. Sometimes I do better, I think so, because they tell me' (2005: 97). May Sem's words convey the sense in which 'cultural survival' is a 'carrying on' (of power, and, just as ambiguously, of 'culture'); they also convey the fear of psychosis as her awareness of her incorporation is heightened by its traumatic context. The dance has become associated with remembering those who trained her, to the extent that she feels infantilized – 'like a child, a baby,' she says, her words echoing the discussion in the previous section – as the one subjected through power is indeed and repeatedly 'in the place of' the child. Each citation is a repetition of training that simultaneously brings with it the repeated memory of those who died. A defiant but sorrowful celebration, the performance is not simply a repetition of the same but a complex mode of situated response.[8] For the Sems, dance becomes the vehicle through which Ben and May perform *answers* for their individual survival, and that of Khmer culture. This 'answerability'[9] is entwined with a complex accountability in which, as Vivian Patraka suggests, the doing/performance is always accountable to the 'thing gone' (1999: 7),[10] while because for the Sems their embodied knowledge has come to account in some way for their own survival, their sense of responsibility is multiplied.

In the Sems' dance there are several 'bodies' performatively engaged. The dancing body exhibits its rigorous training in technique, and in this it carries on the training (the gift and responsibilities) of 'tradition', while the dancer engaged in the performance is supposed to become the embodiment of 'Apsaras', the celestial dancers who guard the heavens and mediate between the sacred and the secular through their dances. Writes Hamara: 'In representing and ventriloquizing the Apsara ideal the body of the dancer becomes the narrative container of the cosmos, a microcosm of myriad nuanced interrelationships between the physical and the spiritual' (2005: 102). Then, on a more prosaic level, there is the refugee-survivor body who in his or her performance offers an ambiguous, non-spoken answer to the past, not just a living memorial but as evidence of cultural survival, exhibiting the fragile promise of the future survival for these traditions within their new contexts.[11] There was, Hamera argues, an acute tension between the 'utopian antiquity' of Khmer dance and the trauma that the Sems deployed dance to 'answer', suggesting also the tension between different meanings in a simultaneous embodiment. When Elin Diamond, recalling Butler's discussions of drag in *Gender Trouble* (1990), suggests that 'the body is never fully subsumed in impersonation' (1997: 180), this incomplete submersion is not to be comprehended as between the real and the acted, the before and the after, but between different simultaneous modes of embodiment as the body moves through necessarily different sets of relations. Likewise, the Sems' movements are not about here and there, now and then, but about different sets of relations which their movements are producing and reproducing.

As a practice of freedom, the dance movements are a mode of resistance and perhaps also a sign of the 'certain vitalism' (1988: 93) that Deleuze finds in Foucault. But they are not of course outside power, being instead a negotiation of it. They do not aim at Freedom – and they certainly do they open up or onto a space of calm satisfaction – but they practise it. This creative, deterritorialized deployment of technique is a strategy of survival, and certainly does not have the status of a model to be emulated. Likewise, although Foucault found himself celebrating the Iranian revolution because he thought he saw there something that might constitute a new relationship between politics and spirituality – a 'political spirituality' (Foucault, in Afary and Anderson, 2005: 209) which turned on a dual 'distrust of legalism' and a 'faith in the creativity of Islam' (Foucault, in Afary and Anderson, 2005: 206) – his later works suggest by contrast that practices of freedom are exactly the attempt to conduct one's practices *within* the relations of power and *without* the 'utopia' or 'ideal' (Foucault, in Afary and Anderson, 2005: 206) which he reported talk of in Iran in those much criticized articles.[12]

The second and third volumes of *The History of Sexuality* consider how, in the study of ancient texts, one might glimpse a kind of resistance that was precisely a question of a certain 'spirituality' (1997/1984: 294), but here, in the texts of the fourth century BC and the first two centuries AD, cleared of its later association with future religious developments.[13] In a late interview Foucault reflected on how spirituality – which he understood as 'the subject's attainment of a certain mode of being and the transformations that the subject must carry out on itself to attain this mode of being' (1997/1984: 294) – had been eclipsed by a philosophy that since Descartes' *Meditations* had shifted to concern itself with the attempt to sustain a mode of being that only ever seeks 'knowledge' and that defines the subject through its ability to attain knowledge (1997/1984: 294). It is not as if a spirituality is recovered by simply rereading the ancient texts, but there is certainly for Foucault a sense in which the practices of freedom he studied there threw light on the inevitability of living within power relations, and of finding a mode of being – of acting, of surviving – within the lines of the *dispositif*.[14] In Volume 2, Foucault explains that the context in which he wished to speak of an arts of existence was a system of gross inequalities: 'Their sexual ethics, from which our own derives in part, rested on a harsh system of inequalities and constraints (particularly in connection with women and slaves); but it was problematized in thought as the relationship, for a free man, between the exercise of his freedom, the forms of his power, and his access to truth' (1985: 253). By considering the problematization, Foucault suggests, the ancient texts indicate that to care for oneself was understood as the proper (ethical) practice of freedom. One had to show oneself not to be a slave of another city, or of those governing you or your own passions (for food, for sex, for beauty, for wealth). '[I]n antiquity' explained

Foucault, 'ethics as the conscious practice of freedom has revolved around this fundamental imperative: take care of yourself!' (1997/1984: 285). If the good, the exemplary, man exercises power without becoming a slave to his desires to be all dominating, this care for his 'self' will also mean that he will not dominate others. It is only later, Foucault argues, that the idea that love of the self will lead to immorality appears, and with it the idea that renunciation of the self is the prime form of care of the self (1997/1984).[15]

I rehearse these well-known arguments here to remind us that performativity has no compatibility with a notion of resistance figured as the avoidance of the lines of power relations. Like Foucault's arguments in the later volumes of *The History of Sexuality*, like Butler's arguments in *Excitable Speech*, there is only ever a working with and even along the lines of the various *dispositifs* within which one is situated and constituted. The Sems' dance does not escape power, but their exemplary performance of it 'answers'. Their embodiment not only confirms the effects of a training, but problematizes it in the reterritorialized context of historical events and geopolitical movements. These then are the complex issues at stake in thinking through the promise of 'performativity'; these are the preconditions with which one begins an analysis of ethics and politics, of difference and the possibility of critique.

CHAPTER 2

Genealogy, Generation and Partiality

In many ways the concept of performativity is set, in principle, against a conception of lineage or generational connection. Indeed, the thrust of the argument is precisely opposed to those who might insist upon the importance of such concerns. For the notion of performativity insists that any apparent continuity across time and space be treated suspiciously, that it be, analytically speaking, punctuated and fragmented, understood as a fragile accomplishment achieved through processes of citation and repetition. As we have seen in Chapter 1, the whole weight of this understanding of the constitution of the subject is to focus attention on the constellation of forces in the midst of which the subject emerges. To seek to comprehend the subject as genealogically delivered, therefore, is seemingly to revert to a mode of thinking cast off by this understanding, one akin to the assertion of interiority: apolitical, naturalistic, naïve and ultimately dangerous. The historical association of such modes of thought with racist, xenophobic and fascistic enterprises stands as a stark warning. However, on the other hand, there is often a sense that the subject stands ultimately quite alone as with the image of the individual body caught within the cell of the Panopticon; indeed the diagram of power sustains that effect in order to render 'cases' from the group on which to construct a generalizable knowledge of the 'type'. Surely this solitude is untenable as an image of how individuals stand in relation to power, indicating only the *desire* of a power that cannot be wholly efficacious. This impression of isolation seems to have been exacerbated rather than lessened, as well it might have been, by Foucault's later volumes in the history of sexuality where the notion of an 'arts of existence' promoted a sense that one might take one's life and seek to act within and between the interstices of power relations in order to adopt the most exemplary path, ethically speaking. It is in contrast to this sense of the subject as a somewhat isolated achievement in relation to power relations, then, that this chapter takes a particular turn from the argument of the last. However, its motivation is not to correct this isolation per se. Rather, it is to follow a point that I discussed in Chapter 1. That is, it presses the point that at the heart of the performativity 'thesis' is the assertion of a paradoxically constitutive plurality. When Jean-Luc Nancy (2000) makes the point that

'Being-with is being's own-most problem', or when Judith Butler (1997b) explores the conditions of possibility of the subject as formed in dependency that she both likens to and sees rooted in the attachments of the infant, both set a train of thought that I take up here in relation to generational connection. For if genealogy as a Foucauldian methodology locates the subject within the twists and turns of history, the emphasis on plurality might just as logically pose the issue of genealogy in the sense of generations or kinship. But to re-enter an exploration of the familial domain, or kinship more broadly, as one of the non-necessary but primary sites at and within which this kernel of plurality must be negotiated, one must proceed cautiously, and one must attend to the dangers with which I here began, since there is of course the danger that the performativity thesis collapses under the weight of that to which it is opposed, that it surrenders its analyses to a psychology or politically speaking, to the most reactionary of stances.

The Challenge of the Flesh

Jonathan and Daniel Boyarin (1993, 1995) have similarly suggested that any attempt to speak of genealogy in the sense of kinship as a mode of theorizing group identities tends to be overwhelmed or usurped by implications of racism. This reaction to the introduction of issues of genealogy is to be understood, they argue, as a legacy of Pauline Christianity in which spiritual kinship has come to trump any articulation of literal descent. This is the context within which one can comprehend the well-meaning commentator who favours individualist, voluntarist communities over anything that begins with the flesh. In the seemingly radical embrace of elective affinities, an embrace whose motivations are good, therefore, Boyarin and Boyarin find a more conservative continuity in so far as, they suggest, the 'valorisation of any kind of elective and affective connection between people over against the claims of physical kinship is deeply embedded in the Platonic value system Europe has largely inherited from Paul' (1993: 702). In Paul, all believers in Christ become of one body, an allegorical genealogy in which 'things of the body are less important than things of the spirit' (1993: 695). The effect of this Pauline legacy, therefore, is that the carnal is devalued in relation to spiritual life. To come together in spirit is regarded as the most progressive route. There has, however, been a Jewish counter-discourse to this legacy, argue Boyarin and Boyarin, one that has given supreme value to literal descent from Abraham. Exploring the implications of this counter-discourse, their work attempts to respond to the trend within leftist and anti-racist philosophy to relegate any existing community to a world that we 'have lost or never existed' (1993: 698),[1] and where 'the physical connection of common descent from Abraham and the embodied practices with which that genealogy is marked off as difference are rejected in favour of a connection between people based on individual re-creation and entry *de novo* into a community of common belief' (1993: 695). In other words, and to extrapolate from their concern with Jewish understandings, they consider the possibility that it may be feasible to speak of one's genealogical positionality in relation to identity without speaking as if there were anything automatic or natural about the link between the two.

Their thoughts about how one might begin to think about generational connections and commitments through the consideration of how genealogy is performatively recognized guide me here, as does Paul Gilroy's provocative work (2000) which continues his attempts to pursue anti-racist thinking in ways that challenge forms of identity as sameness. Their complementary tasks – linked most clearly via the term 'diaspora' – explore the modes of commemoration through which the work of maintaining identities occurs. For Gilroy the term 'diaspora' enables one to speak of a dynamic lived consciousness; it is a term that escapes the pitfalls of essentialist thought by giving due attention to the complexities of the imagination that links and crosses space and time as had black bodies in slavery and as various commodities do in contemporary life. For Boyarin and Boyarin the example of the Jewish diaspora has a particular pertinence not least due to the insistence on bodily connection and embodied practice within the experience of diaspora. In their writings, as we will see, there is in short the possibility of thinking identities as *both* given and created.

Inserting a discussion of Levinas's writings into this problematic is unsettling because his arguments challenge the perspectives from which much progressive work in cultural theory is written and with which it seems comfortable. Indeed, his arguments at this juncture are such that, despite much current interest in Levinasian ethics, and in Derrida's usage thereof, his entrance may prove unwelcome. Nevertheless, I want to stage this meeting, because in some crucial ways Levinas points to the difficulty of these issues concerning embodied connectedness that Boyarin and Boyarin and other theorists of diaspora raise, ones that many cultural theorists, for good reasons, tend to set aside. Levinas is of interest here because he directly addressed the issue of how forms of connectedness are felt *as one's very being is felt*. And this most keenly, where the affective disposition towards alterity within the subject, as the structure or pattern of subjectivity[2] has a quality such that 'existing itself becomes double' (Levinas 1987: 92). This remark is made in reference to paternity, which is, I am suggesting, one articulation of the term 'chaining' that he uses elsewhere and that has been my provocation in this context. My turn to Levinas, then, is born out of a concern that I share with Boyarin and Boyarin, namely that there might be a danger of moving too quickly to a position whereby the desire to refigure identity politics in non-essentialist ways means a refusal or denial of the connectedness, the multiplicity of existing, that is generational or genealogical attachment, a move that, as it were, surrenders the term 'identity' to identity politics. That is, the attempt to move beyond identity politics by positing identity as violent per se (attractive though such a proposition is in such persuasive articulations as that of the philosopher David Wood) may relinquish the opportunity to pursue reasons for the *tenacity* of those forms of group identity, and transform itself into a way of speaking that cannot imagine its audience except through appeals to a future body-politic that its speech intends both to address and to bring about. In other words, it feels like an abdication to write as if the world were archaic and has yet to catch up with the values espoused in political philosophical tracts – bemoaning 'we can write beyond identity, if only the world could live beyond it?' – without attempting to understand why living beyond identity, is, for many, neither attractive nor conceivable. By contrast, might there not be ways of exploring the notion of cultural identity that acknowledge embodied identities but understand them as performative achievements that are attached to others in ways that are partial but not identitarian. Too often the felt modalities of the temporal are rendered inadmissible as if present political machinations of political processes were based on opinions, ones formed just now or yesterday. The flattening out of democratic models attempts to ignore the depth of the various 'positions' that meet there; and these positions are 'deep' because *felt*, and as such they are (frequently but not always) *bodily*, in ways that I mean to discuss. These positions are not of course essential, ontological or inevitable identities, and have a constancy only due their reiteration.[3] But it is the *sense* of identity, its *felt embodiment*, and the inextricability and undesirability of removing one's attachment to identity, that is of concern here.

To state the problem via a different literature, Hannah Arendt, to whom we will return below, argued that in politics 'the world is at stake' so that political subjects need to sublate the personal for the sake of the world; but what is it that makes an individual care for something as abstract as 'the world'? What is the adventure of the personal that involves one in the world, and how are partialities, those connections that one feels are tied to oneself as a specific subjectivity in one way or another, that constitute oneself, to be reconciled with the ethics of being one among many, the multiplicities that make up 'the world'? My problem is how to be able to think about belonging as performative routedness[4] in a way that maintains the emphasis on the complex cultural processes by which identities are thoroughly constructed, while simultaneously acknowledging the weight of genealogy, the sense of identities and partialities that people feel as a mode of their very embodiment.

Indeed, if Levinas is to be believed, without that acknowledgement, one may contribute to a situation in which the celebration of an 'era of non-identity', a term used by Helene Cixious, actually promotes, or at least renders itself unable to challenge, the worst and most virulent of identity politics. (How big an 'if' this sentence contains! Levinas states his argument boldly, seems to stand by its sentiment in later years, and I shall follow its logic here as an exercise in provocation rather than as an act of affiliation, for the argument is certainly contentious). As we shall see, this was the argument of Levinas's early piece on Hitlerism published in 1933 and again in 1990 with a preface in which Levinas wrote that his intention had been to warn philosophy that it has to protect itself from leaving open the appeal of racist movements that would capitalize on those who with the most laudable intentions – the pursuit of liberal democracy – wished away genealogically conferred connections. The challenge, then, is to maintain my sympathies for a notion of identities as forms of belonging, spatially and temporally performed within self-constitutive webs of power and knowledge, while appreciating the important nuances and challenges that Levinas's arguments pose for that conception.

To gloss the manoeuvres of my argument: I am going to use Levinas's later work on paternity, specifically the sections of *Totality and Infinity* where he addresses fecundity and paternity, to develop an argument that to some extent 'answers' his earlier piece on Hitlerism. Both of these can be regarded as pieces on embodiment and generational attachments; both complicate the question of identity in self–other relations since they reach beyond the inter-human order where each individual is imagined as absolutely independent one of the other, and attend instead on those relationships that are neither simply of identification nor of alterity, that is, those of genealogical connection. My focus, then, is on the forms of duality, even multiplicity, that accompany the discontinuity of generations. In short, I want to argue that one can develop out of Levinas's arguments a position whereby one can acknowledge an embodied relation to the past – a chaining – which nonetheless, cannot be figured as a determinative weight on the present nor on the future; the future concerns me – and more forcefully than this, one could say in Levinasian language it *is* mine, it is *my* adventure, even though it must never be confused with me – but nonetheless, the future cannot be regarded as in any sense *fated* because of its connection with me nor my connections with the past.

The Attachment to Identity: Levinas's Notion of Chaining

Contemporary theoretical explorations of the subject and processes of subject-ification have explored, within a number of theoretical registers, the relationship of the emergent subject to his or her conditions of possibility as one of both subjection and necessity. For example, as we have seen in Chapter 1, Judith Butler has explored the attachment that the subject feels to the relations of power that produce him or her, a passionate (positive or negative) attachment, moreover, born out of the desire to maintain existence itself. The subject is produced as an effect of reiteration, and the subject by necessity reiterates itself in the terms of the constituting power, even if in that need for repetition there is the possibility of rearticulation and resignification. The possibility of using the incompleteness of the constitution of the subject, the temporal disjunctures, the remainders and the 'gaps' between the various sites and discourses that are assembled in that constitution of that subject, is the possibility of political hope. Thus the attachment to identity is inevitable but not essential nor unchanging; any process of dis-attachment is, moreover, very likely to pass through attachment.

In Chapter 3 of *The Psychic Life of Power* on 'Subjection, Resistance, Resignification' (1997b: 83–105), Butler's position speaks of identity abstractly, but where she reaches for an example it is the example of the child. The child's attachment to the parents is a productive power that the child mustn't 'see' because his/her identity (as a separate individual) is based on the denial of desire for those contingent power relations. Thus although she clearly has issues of gender and sexuality as well as ethnicity in mind, Butler's use of the image of the child as an example and an analogy means that the issue of generation is simultaneously thrown up. How does this notion of an attachment to the power regimes that constitute one's identity relate to Levinas's arguments, where the focus is on the question of what we would now term ethnicity and the question of 'chaining'?

In 1933 Levinas argued that Hitlerism's attraction at the time was, in part, due to its appeal to people's felt embodiment. As opposed to a Christian tradition in which the body has been detached from the soul, the former figured as a mere container of the latter, Hitlerism articulated a sense of 'chaining'. While liberalism mimicked the separation of body and soul, with the notion of the will substituting for the soul, Hitlerism rooted itself in the simplicity of the body, its sensations and its connections to others. The power of this stance was that it managed to convince people that the disappointment they were feeling in political philosophies was answered in its distorted version of a subtle truth. That is, that each person's identity is felt in the body; it is bodily sensation that most intimately ties one to one's own being, as in the experience of pain, where the spirit or will fights desperately but remains, inescapably, in the body. Beginning with a conception of identity as embodied, Hitlerism provided a new discourse in which embodied connections were exploited to their full, proclaiming as it did that 'to be truly oneself does not mean taking flight once more above contingent events that always remain foreign to the Self's freedom; on the contrary, it means becoming aware of the ineluctable original chain that is unique to our bodies, and above all, accepting this chaining' (Levinas 1990/1933: 69).

Levinas contrasts Hitlerism with liberal political philosophies, which still render the body insignificant, elevating instead the notion of reason and the general will so that a dualism remains, subordinating the body to an abstract identification. Just as would Adorno and Horkheimer (1986/1944), Levinas argued that liberalism had disappointed; its promise had not been fulfilled and people's sense of the future as open to the people's collective will did not provide any comfort. Hitlerism relied upon returning a sense of embodiment that brought with it a sense of history as determined by a higher law. If democracy relied upon a sense of the future as open to the choices for the individual, as if liberalism had, as had Christianity, the ability to tame the past through the triumph of a disembodied spirit, then Hitlerism relied upon appealing to a sense of that history and embodiment. The logic of Hitlerism insists on a sense of *chaining*, on a sense that the future is not open, the spirit or will is not free of the body, but is instead always bound to its past, anchored in flesh and blood. The choice of the citizen, under this logic, is not one that is freed from the body, nor is it one that can be altered in the future. For the person accepting his or her chaining to his body and the past, truth is not achieved through processes of rational and detached thought: it is *'under the weight of his whole existence*, which includes facts on which there is no going back, that man will say his yes or his no' (1990/1933: 70, with Levinas's masculine pronoun).

A further corollary of this fascist doctrine, Levinas argues, is that the idea of community, under such a formulation, can only come about by blood. Rational or mystical communion between spirits – indeed, any form of community that attempts to deny the body or re-create dualisms of the mind/spirit kind – is positioned as suspicious and ultimately as untruthful. Furthermore, the truth that National Socialism upheld was not to be shared or 'taught' exactly, for that would be to engage in another form of equalization, or, reading Levinas back on himself here, to reimpose an idea of spirit by making a community through (rational, read spiritual) conviction. The universal truth of consanguinity is characterized not by propagation of an idea, but by force, by expansion. Those who submit are universalized by the propagation of war and conquest; even as they become forcibly 'included', they do not become equal.

Levinas's point, as he says in his 1990 preface to this early piece, is that philosophy has to protect itself from leaving open this appeal of racist movements. The philosopher's task is to find a way to speak and validate the experience of embodiment, and the fact of genealogical connection, without replicating dualisms that will not hold and that, upon their dissolution, enable pernicious political philosophies to gain credence. How then to think about embodied relations to genealogy but in ways that do not merely accept that chaining nor elevate it into a determinative force and moral principle?

Boyarin and Boyarin have been exploring attachment somewhat differently, but with an emphasis that might be understood as a response to Levinas's provocations here in so far as they argue that the constitution of oneself as a Jewish subject, a subjection and subjectification that is also highly gendered and patriarchal (see Boyarin, 1997), is an embodied constitution that involves *practices* rather than spiritual communion. They argue that Judaism has provided a critique of Pauline traditions through its attention to genealogy and embodiment: 'the insistence on the value of bodily connection and embodied practice that is emblematic of Judaism since Paul thus has significant critical power vis-à-vis the isolating and disembodying direction of Western idealist philosophies' (1993: 705–6). Appropriately enough, then, it is as if Boyarin and Boyarin find the answer to Levinas's problem within those who were persecuted by the National Socialist ideology that Levinas was concerned about in this piece written even before the full horrors of Hitler's power could have been imagined. There is within Judaism, they argue, a powerful example of how one might speak about embodiment without determination and genealogy without racism, that is, because one can understand Judaism as achieved through practices that maintain rather than rely upon genealogical connection. They emphasize in their various writings that Judaism is a practice and it is also in their view important to regard it as a *changing* context for the constitution of 'Jewish subjects'. It is a 'changing same'.

Gilroy elaborates Leroi Jones's notion of the 'changing same' thus:

> The same is present but how can we imagine it as something other than an essence generating the merely accidental? Iteration is the key to this process. The same is retained without needing to be reified. It is ceaselessly reprocessed. It is maintained and modified in what becomes a determinedly non-traditional tradition, for this is not tradition as closed or simple repetition. Invariably promiscuous, diaspora and the politics of commemoration it specifies, challenge us to apprehend mutable forms that can redefine the idea of culture through a reconciliation with movement and complex, dynamic variation. (2000: 129–30)

The chaining, then, is genealogically conferred and embodied, but it is a practice and as such it is contingent, contextualized, intermittent and temporal in the sense that it requires reiteration. Although, and even *because*, there will be those who would refuse this contingency, 'chained' identity can be thought as non-essentialist and as performative. Thus one has Gilroy's examples in *The Black Atlantic* where he argues that diaspora names the syncretic compound formations that entail the reiteration of connections but that are never simply duplications. One is speaking here of 'a mix, a hybrid, recombinant form, *that is indebted to its 'parent' cultures* but remains assertively and insubordinately a bastard' (Gilroy, 1997: 323).

Pursuing this line of thought, Boyarin and Boyarin argue that it is a mistake for radical theorists to understand their work as working against racism when it figures ideal future communities as 'writing themselves', as it were. For Jean-Luc Nancy, they write, the 'necessary fiction that grounds the insistent specialness of the existent communal group is an irreducible component of community and at the same time is necessarily pernicious in its effects' (1993: 698). For them, such grounding fictions are not necessarily pernicious. Indeed, despite Nancy's intentions, the concept of a 'community to come' could be seen to partake in a dismissal of Judaism even as it applauds it. When Nancy quotes Blanchot's idea that 'the Jews incarnate the refusal of myth' – an ambiguous quotation because one is not sure if the argument is that the Jews really do as such or if this was itself one of Hitler's myths – Nancy suggests that the Jew represented 'before "he" was annihilated' that which 'we' must let come, which we must let write itself. However, either, if it is so, their refusal of myth becomes that which must be everywhere repeated, eclipsing the existent differences in an attempt to promote freedom from myth. (That is, the cry 'let us all be like the Jews!' ultimately erases their difference.) Or, if the notion that the Jews exist free from myth is itself understood as one of Hitler's myths, Boyarin and Boyarin argue that Nancy's point is that it is necessary to work against the myth of the freedom from myth. In this task, the Jewish diaspora might be particularly interesting, especially in relation to the myth of autochthony. An anti-Zionist Jewish stance, therefore, that allows a particular place to 'generational connection and its attendant anamnestic responsibilities and pleasures' might, they suggest, give some insight into what a flexible and non-hermetic critical Jewish identity might be (1993: 701). In Boyarin and Boyarin's hands therefore, the 'changing same' makes sense only when understood alongside literal genealogy, and their argument is that that fact can be reintroduced without subtending what Gilroy terms the 'tyrannies of unanimism' (2000: 207–37).

This is to suggest therefore that there might, even within the 'performativity' thesis, be a place for the consideration of generational, carnal connection. Properly considered, the subject can be comprehended as emerging within a diagram of power relations that need not disallow the genealogically conferred to enter consideration.

But there remains a further important issue in relation to the question of 'chaining', one which is possibly more difficult. This is the question of partiality, understood here as the value that one places on those with whom one is genealogically entwined. Levinas is known for regarding the subject as disposed toward the other, since ethics, for him, revolves around the question of the responsibility for the other's response (as I will discuss further in Chapter 3). But reading him with the question of generations in mind complicates his thought, and reposes the questions that I have been discussing thus far. That is, these same questions have also to be posed with a futural dimension, and with the figure of the child more clearly within the frame. And with the figure of the child the political and ethical questions arise again, this time understood as the tension between partialities and multiplicities.

The Child

> Existing itself becomes double.
> Levinas, *Time and the Other*

Interestingly, it seems the concerns of this early piece on Hitlerism find an echo in Levinas's later work, where he attempts to find a way to speak about genealogical connection with the future through the discontinuity of the generations between parent and child. In the section of *Totality and Infinity* which I will discuss here, Levinas begins with the phenomenology of eros, where he suggests that erotic desire, unlike a need which can be sated, is fed by its satisfaction, and repeatedly seeks what is 'not yet' – a beyond the future. Levinas means to contrast this sense of the 'not yet' with a relation to the future based on possibilities that might be anticipated and to some extent grasped. Erotic love could not be said to grasp, but rather in the caress, there is a foraging, a searching, 'soliciting what slips away as though it were not yet' (1969: 257–8).[5] In the relation between lovers there is a movement toward the 'not yet' beyond the future of possibles; a 'not yet more remote than the future'. Voluptuosity is the affirmation of the other as sentient, as though 'one same sentiment were substantially common to me and to the other – and not as two observers have a common landscape or two thinkers a common idea' (1969: 265). It is at this point that Levinas surprises the reader by describing the non-unification of erotic desire in terms of the 'not yet child'. In the unparalleled conjuncture of identification, in the transubstantiation, 'the same and the other are not united but precisely – beyond every possible project, beyond every meaningful and intelligent power – engender the child' (1969: 266). At this point one might enter a discussion of Levinas's heterosexism, the privileging of a certain implicit image of erotic desire, but this time I wish to move with him because my interest is really in what comes next.

Levinas states that 'already the relation with the child – coveting the child, both other and myself – takes form in voluptuosity, to be accomplished in the child himself' (1969: 266). That is, as I interpret Levinas here, in the relationship with the Beloved, in the delight that identifies spontaneously with the other in his or her sentient being, there is the spectre, the hope (and/or the terror, perhaps) of a future: the not-yet child.

Moving from a discussion of the not-yet child to the relationship with the actual child, Levinas presents an argument where the relationship of paternity is understood as a form of identification that contains an important caveat, a distinction, within it. Speaking of paternity – the relationship between father and son – Levinas expands upon a relationship where the father 'discovers himself not only in the gestures of his son but in his substance and his unicity. My child is a stranger (Isaiah 49) but a stranger who is not only mine, for he is me. He is me a stranger to myself ... no anticipation represents him nor ... projects him' (1969: 267). In *Time and the Other*, Levinas had spoken of paternity as a pluralist existing: 'Paternity is not simply the renewal of the father in the son and the father's merger with him, it is also the father's exteriority in relation to the son, a pluralist existing' (1987: 92). Thus – and here we come to the most interesting of formulations for our present purposes – 'paternity remains a self-identification, but also a distinction within identification' (1969: 267). Later, he states again: 'Paternity is a relation with a stranger who while being Other (Isaiah 49) is me, a relation of the I with a self which yet is not me' a structure that, he adds, goes 'beyond the biologically empirical' (1969: 277).

Correlatively, the relationship to the future in paternity is one that is irreducible to the graspable, the possible – it is a relationship to the future that is both mine and not-mine; Levinas names it fecundity.

> Fecundity encloses a duality of the Identical. It does not denote all that I can grasp – my possibilities; it denotes my future, which is not a future of the same ... *And yet it is my adventure still*, and consequently my future in a very new sense, despite the discontinuity. (1969: 268)

And importantly, this is where Levinas contrasts the relation with the child with a relation of power:

> In power the indetermination of the possible does not exclude the reiteration of the I, which in venturing toward this indeterminate future falls back on its feet, and, riveted to itself, acknowledges its transcendence to be merely illusory and its freedom to delineate but a fate... . In fecundity the tedium of this repetition ceases; the I is other and young, yet the ipseity that ascribed to it its meaning and its orientation in being is not lost in this renouncement of self. Fecundity continues history without producing old age. Infinite time does not bring an eternal life to an ageing subject; it is better across the discontinuity of generations, punctuated by the inexhaustible youths of the child. (1969: 268)

Thus in voluptuosity, there is a duality, both fusion and distinction (1969: 270). In paternity by contrast there is the resolution of erotic love, but there remains discontinuity, for in paternity 'the future still refers to the personal from which it is nonetheless liberated: it is the child, mine in a certain sense or, more exactly, *me, but not myself; it does not fall back upon my past to fuse with it and delineate a fate*' (1969: 271–2, italics added). The openness to the future that is paternity is a discontinuity that does not break with the self – 'it is my adventure still' – so that it is what Levinas had called in *Time and the Other* a 'pluralist existing' (1987: 92) in which there is 'a duality in existence, a duality that concerns the very existing of each subject. Existing itself becomes double'

(1987: 92). At the end of that book Levinas stresses that he has been occupied as a 'main goal' with emphasizing that 'alterity is not purely and simply the existence of another freedom next to mine' (1987: 92) for in such an understanding the 'coexistence of several freedoms is a multiplicity that leaves the unity of each intact or else this multiplicity unites into a general will' (1987: 92). There is not a dissolution of self into the future figured as society or community as a 'mere' plurality, for

> Fecundity is part of the very drama of the I. The intersubjective reached across the notion of fecundity opens up a place where the I is divested of its tragic egoity, which turns back to itself, and yet is not purely and simply dissolved into the collective. *Fecundity evinces a unity that is not opposed to multiplicity but in the precise sense of the term, engenders it* (1969: 273).

Between Continuity and Discontinuity

Juxtaposing these arguments of Levinas's concerning paternity and fecundity with the early piece on Hitlerism, suggests a particular reading of the notions of genealogy and generation. How might one think through the discontinuity of generations in these terms, as framing and constraining but without the comfort of directing forms of identities? Certainly the political weight and importance of that thought is emphasized by the prophetic arguments that the young Levinas made about the impotence of liberal thought.

In the model of identification with internal distinction (that of paternity) there can be a discontinuity that does not break from the I. The future is my adventure to be, but one where I journey without returning to the I – even as it issues from my body, takes on my gestures, is me. Levinas says his thoughts on paternity are not about biological relations; and in the early piece on Hitlerism, his point is exactly to think about the intimacy of the I with the body in a way that can challenge those who would reduce genealogical relations and possibilities to the biological or to blood. The gestures, then, need not be thought as inherited genetically, but as a reflection of more social forms of inheritance, that is, of socialization. I am attracted to the idea – even as I struggle with its complexities and potential complicities, and with the poor example that Levinas himself made of it in relation to the state of Israel and the plight of the Palestinians (see Hand, 1989) – that the multiplicity of the future concerns me, is mine, is my adventure but is also not me; and how that notion operates with the argument that there is an embodied relation to the past – a chaining – which nonetheless, cannot be figured as a determinative weight in the present – the future is not fated because of its connection with me nor my connections with the past.

Thus there is a need to acknowledge the past as informing the present, but that present needs to be understood as constituted through dynamic performative presentation. Both Boyarin and Boyarin and Gilroy emphasize that their concern is with the processes, with *how* these diasporic connections come to matter in the present. These involve the way that one's past and one's belonging to it is performed culturally and socially, the forms of remembrance that are practised, as well as how one's obligations to the future are framed. Within such an exploration, one would have attention on how genealogy may be made to matter in children's futures in the various domains in which that relationship is constituted, in other words the ways that individuals are invited into and implicated in the continuity of their ethnicity, religion or nation. Clearly, how notions of generations past and future are *deployed*, that is, the ways they are made visible, intelligible and communicable, bring the genealogy–generation couplet both into the aesthetics of existence and to a politics of multiplicity. The presentation of self, in other words, involves a presentation, remembrance or anticipation of others who are deemed related in some way to that presentation – informing, influencing, creating it – such that an aesthetics of belonging becomes also a question of ethics, due to the discontinuity that its enactment both conceals and reveals. That is, the having to enact – even in circumstances where identity is marked on the body (as in Boyarin and Boyarin's example of male circumcision in their chapter 'Self-Exposure as Theory' (1995)) – reveals that there is a discontinuity that the enacting attempts to conceal. In that presentation of self, that 'aesthetics of existence', however, one is necessarily positioning oneself with respect to others and hence within an ethical frame. Each generation arrives into a world peopled by many others, and due to the unique nature of their context, each generation faces these questions anew.

Due to this *multiplicity* of the future that one engenders, these are not only aesthetic and ethical questions but deeply political ones, for any influence that one has on how continuities are understood and articulated is also an influence on the means by which differences are understood and articulated. But even as one is obliged to understand the present as forming the contexts within which the future may be rendered intelligible, there can be no prescriptive element in one's relation to the future. Thus the question becomes: how does one acknowledge both chaining and discontinuity, as one is obliged to do, such that neither is denied but neither becomes an attempt to prescribe, discriminate, direct or contain? What is the relation to the future given the ethical and political issues of accepting both chaining and discontinuities within identification?

Wherever the discontinuity is denied by attempting to contain another's adventure (freedom and life) as *wholly* mine, as wholly chained, one can say that there is an attempt to control the possibilities of the future. Levinas might say that this would be a narcissistic strategy where one seeks to 'capture, thematize, reduce, use and thus to annihilate or annul the other' (de Vries, 1997:

16). An overemphasis on discontinuity, however, might return us to the problems identified by Boyarin and Boyarin in relation to the well-meaning theorist who simply rules out genealogical connection by Pauline wishful thinking.

This is the tension we are left with, one that can be illustrated by the sense
in which one can stage a peculiar meeting on this question between Levinas's
concerns and those of Hannah Arendt. The discontinuity that is the adult's
relationship to the child is exactly what Arendt, writing some thirty years after
Levinas's Hitlerism piece and a decade or so before *Totality and Infinity*,
wanted to protect, and for somewhat similar political reasons to Levinas. For
Arendt, totalitarianism attempted to quell the distance between generations,
to mould the child and crush the newness of each generation because their
capacity to begin anew was threatening. For her, what is crucial to protect is
the child's development of his/her capacity to begin, since it is at the heart of
freedom.

But Arendt's position led her to her peculiar stance on the racial desegregation of schools in the South in the 1950s.[6] Counter-intuitively, she argued
against desegregation, for a mixture of reasons that can be understood as
stemming in large part from the notion that generational discontinuities
should be kept discontinuous. She saw the state's attempt to reconfigure the
racial distribution of schools and children's racialized patterns of socializing
through this manoeuvre as almost akin to a dictatorial intervention that was
attempting to force what should be natural and freely chosen. She argued that
the social institution of the school was one where children should be allowed
to mix with whomsoever they chose, and that forcing the black children to
attend the white school where there was so much open hostility to their doing
so, was to ask children to solve the problem of racism – something that adults
themselves were unable to do. Her argument was, in part, that children should
be allowed to develop their social (and later, political) skills and relations
without such intervention. Children need the private sphere in order to foster
their individuality, and to protect their capacity for freedom, read as the
capacity to begin, on which future democratic politics will depend. Making the
children attend a previously all-white school was, she argued, an intervention
that distorted the private realm, interfered with their rights to free association,
and was inappropriate to fostering children's individualities.

The problem with Arendt's position can be understood as stemming, in the
terms of our discussion here, from her sense that it *is* somehow possible to
remove oneself completely from the future. But to pretend that the child exists
in isolation from the parents and their opinions, traditions, prejudices, that
s/he can freely associate and develop individuality as if s/he were completely
discontinuous from the parents and parental generation, is disingenuous on
Arendt's part. *For where discontinuity is overemphasized there is an abdication of
responsibility akin to those politics that stem from an overemphasis on continuity. For*

in the gestures of the son one sees the father. It is discontinuous, but it is my adventure still. One *cannot* remove oneself from the future, as if that were an anti-fascist manoeuvre. That would be to attempt to give up the child/not-yet child, and to deny the sense in which the present is the context for the future's intelligibility.

The issue, therefore, is how to live between these two extremes – the attempt to remove oneself completely from the child, and the attempt to assimilate the child to oneself – that each carry dangers. To abandon the child completely to its own adventure is to deny responsibility for one's own ethical position, for one's own involvement in the child, for oneself 'in' the child. So too the incorporation of the child completely into oneself, or even into an abstract totality – the nation, tradition, religion – is to attempt to make continuous a discontinuity, and would be another form of violence to the child.

Concluding Remarks: Sacrifice, Partiality, Ethics

Ralph Ellison disagreed with Arendt's analysis of what happened in relation to the desegregation of schools in Little Rock. In an interview with Ralph Warren, collected in Warren's *Who Speaks for the Negro?*, Ellison argues 'one of the important clues to the meaning of [American Negro] experience lies in the idea, the *ideal* of sacrifice' (Warren, 1966: 343). Arendt had failed to grasp this, he argued, in her 'Reflections' article:

> she has absolutely no conception of what goes on in the minds of Negro parents when they send their kids through those lines of hostile people ... they are aware of overtones of a rite of initiation which such events actually constitute for the child, a confrontation of the terrors of social life with all the mysteries stripped away. And in the outlook of many of those parents (who wish that the problem didn't exist), the child is expected to face the terror and contain his fear and anger *precisely* because he is a Negro American. Thus he's required to master the inner tensions created by his racial situation, and if he gets hurt – then his is one more sacrifice. It is a harsh requirement, but if he fails this basic test, his life will be even harsher. (Warren, 1966: 344)[7]

Ellison's argument is reminiscent of a certain reading of the story of Abraham's willingness to sacrifice his beloved son Isaac when requested by God. It is because of the love of the child, and the need to make a good world for that child, that the child will be put through suffering, even pain. Some children will be sacrificed because if that risk is not run, there will be no hope for them in the present world, and no hope for a better world. In Derrida's reading of the story of Abraham and Isaac in *The Gift of Death* (1995) he emphasizes the silence that Abraham keeps about his decision to obey God and to sacrifice his son, for whereas we tend to think that responsibility is public accounting of oneself, Abraham's silence and secrecy – that is, his unresponsivity – is what

makes him responsible in the sense of being *singularly* responsible for his decision. Abraham, the most moral and the most immoral of men is, as Kierkegaard
said, a witness and not a teacher. Moreover, to attempt to make a public
account would be to attempt to make God reasonable and thereby to diminish
his very Godliness. 'Abraham cannot speak, because he cannot say that which
would explain everything ... that is an ordeal such that, please note, the ethical
is the temptation' (Kierkegaard, quoted in Derrida, 1995: 61).

The ethical then, Derrida writes, 'can end up making us irresponsible. It is
a temptation, a tendency or a facility that would sometimes have to be refused
in the name of a responsibility that doesn't keep account or give an account'
(1995: 61–2). Perhaps something similar is being argued in Gilroy's *The Black
Atlantic* (1993) when he reads Toni Morrison's *Beloved* in order to argue that
infanticide – this time under conditions of slavery – can suggest where there is
slavery in life, freedom may be anticipated in death. But in Levinas the
problem is that the *singularity* of the relationship to the child, the partiality of
it, one's responsiveness to one's own child, tempts one into the unethical in
the sense of an irresponsiveness to all others. As Derrida puts it 'I cannot
respond to the call, the request, the obligation or even the love of another
without sacrificing the other other, the other others' (1995: 66). Similarly, one
could say that one's responsiveness to one's own traditions or familial connections is a form of partiality that is tempted into the unethical or irresponsible.
Thus the moves to highlight the syncretic or hybridic natures of cultures, the
most hegemonic of cultures included, has been aimed at the unethical consequences that are subtended by an emphasis on the illusory repetition of a
purely given and simply repeated unchanging cultural tradition.

From the point of view of the child there is, according to Levinas, a relationship to fraternity built into filiality – and this might be one line of argument that moves away from this problem – as the child can only be special and
think herself special *by contrast*, as amongst others. The aesthetic, ethical and
political questions that I discussed above are clustered in the modes by which
one articulates one's connections in the face of others. From the point of view
of the adult/parent maybe one could extrapolate that there is, or there needs
to be, a concern with that multiplicity due to one's awareness of one's partiality. The parent as both teacher and witness is obliged to be concerned with
the multiplicity that s/he partially engenders, and is obliged to *foster* the multiplicity as a *condition* or in order to truly maintain the integrity of the love of the
singular (child). This would be a different voicing perhaps of Arendt's refrain
that in politics the world is at stake, not one's own, temporary, involvement in
it.[8] Has not my temporary involvement with the child an obligation to also be
an engagement with the multiple world within which s/he will live after my
departure from it? Is not to ignore that fact to refuse the ethical responsibility
that is bound up with my contribution, through the child, to the political

future? Becoming responsive to others' children, and therefore to others' *partialities*, would mean becoming aware of the fact that, as Derrida writes, despite 'our' stupefied response to Abraham's sacrifice, this is the most common in event the world – the sacrifice of children, and with awful clarity in situations of conflict – so much so that its occurrence no longer constitutes an event. Too often a perversion of caring for the world means that this care morphs into a violence based upon caring for *these* children, or for ones who will be like them, such that in the name of preserving a world, a future is imagined in which only children *like* these could partake. For that, these children must more or less literally put their own lives on the line. Even in the most 'ethical' of motivations, the unethical, or its temptations at least, persist.

Perhaps this version of caring for the future world is ultimately inconclusive, a pronouncement that doesn't satisfactorily answer the various questions that are raised here. Moreover, it probably simply begs the question, merely repeating the dilemmas that have been prompted by Levinas: how to emerge from a situation where, in the moment of the decision, as Derrida puts it, 'what binds me in my singularity to the singularity of the other immediately propels me into the space or risk of absolute sacrifice?' That is, when one responds to the face that 'is' one's own, or to the other that carries one's own gestures (one's ancestors, parent, child) can one truly bear in mind the multiple faces to whom one is not responding? If these brief ruminations on these questions will not aid in answering this ultimate question, suffice it for now that some of the lines of thought that, to my mind, need to be appended to it may have been mapped out here. Not least among these is the question of political affiliations and identifications. For if these articulate themselves as precisely the contexts within which there is the possibility of transcending partiality, they are also quite rightly the site of scepticism about such an endeavour. Indeed, the pursuit of 'the ethical' may not be the best formulation for radical politics. The next chapter explores this issue, returning again to the writings of Levinas to pose another set of questions in this regard, this time taking place within feminism.

CHAPTER 3

Negotiating the Non-ethical: On 'Ethical Feminism'

The unforseeability of the wholly other represents a kind of nemesis to the present that keeps the present off balance and prevents it from acquiring too much prestige.

Caputo, *More Radical Hermeneutics*

From Feminist Ethics to Ethics and Feminism

In so far as feminism's express concern is to mobilize against injustice and, arguably, to see instituted a universal value of equality, it is, like ethics, concerned with the quality of the spaces between people, and with the key ethical questions of responsiveness and responsibility. Indeed, as Drucilla Cornell has argued, the history of feminism has been a series of challenges to re-imagine the values by which human beings live, especially in terms of seeking to have harms that were not regarded as harmful (discrimination against women, sexual violences) seen differently; feminism presents an 'endless challenge to the ethical imagination' (Cornell, 1995: 79). However, there has been of late an increasing amount of work that renders the intimacy between feminism and ethics problematic. Some feminists are now highly sceptical of the possibility of 'an ethical (way of) being' and thus the pursuit of a 'feminist ethics' has been placed under question. This is not to say, however, that the question of ethics could be simply rendered obsolete; feminism cannot abandon the question of ethics *tout court* because feminism's political hope rests upon being able to be confidently responsive and responsible. It would not be hyperbolic to suggest that, currently, it is on the ground of ethics that the possible architecture of that hope is being most hotly debated.

Indeed, although feminist debates on ethics have come a long way from the arguments that had an all-caring female figure at their heart,[1] to speak of the ethics of feminist politics is perhaps something slightly different again. Thus, on the one hand, there has been a healthy scepticism about positing an ethics of or for women; certainly the exploration of ethical intersubjectivity has all but abandoned any sense that women can simply be understood to have a more care-orientated, less rule-orientated ethical capacity than men. Elizabeth Spelman argued some time ago that feminists must not be too quick to 'feel virtuous about attending to the virtues of feeling, the marvel of care' (1991: 229), not least because the history of women's capacities to be inhumane to other women cannot be simply removed from the discussion of ethics. More recently, Bat-Ami Bar On has argued that in the portrayal of the inspirational women within the Palestine/Israel conflict, feminists should take care not to forget the *fragility* of virtue (1998: 48–9, drawing on Davis, 1992 and Nussbaum, 1986), a virtue that may take gendered forms (for example, related to women's lesser involvement in military action or women's roles as teachers of children). Women can be affected by the stresses of war in ways that make them ethico-politically impoverished, unable to think about impassioned struggle without understanding it as necessarily a violent life-and-death struggle and unable to imagine a democratic future peace. She argues that feminists need to turn 'not just to women's resistance to violence for inspiration but also toward a better understanding of the gendered nature of the fragility of women's virtue and its violent undoing' (1998: 52). Certainly these courageous points add to the subtleties of the feminist debate on ethics, one which recognizes that characterizing the quality of the 'space between us' (Cockburn, 1998) has become a complicated endeavour, which must attend to the issues of gender as, if you will, *performative*.[2]

On the other hand, to pose the question of the ethics of feminist politics is to shift the terrain in important ways. It is to change the questions at stake, away from those that have traditionally surrounded the debate on feminism and ethics – how should we imagine an ethical life (such that it will include difference, gender difference as well as further differences?) – to questions about the relationship between ethics and politics. Indeed, it is to open up a set of concerns that have not traditionally been addressed at the site of ethics. These turn less on how we conceive the intersubjective encounter and more on how we understand the political imagination of feminism itself.

In a sense the consideration of the political imagination of feminism has flowed from its attention to ethics. Thus, as feminists have grappled with the possibility of ethical sensibilities that respect differences across geographic distance, within an unequal global economy with its colonial legacies and its continuing uneven forms of development (Jaggar, 2000: 364, summarizing Moser, 1993), or as they have considered environmental ethics (Warren, 1990), they simultaneously raise something of feminism's own desire. That is, to be able to talk of ethics in relation to 'women' in the face of the complexities of women's differences within countries and across the globe, is also to question how feminism imagines its politics – the temporalities, the affects, the desires – at stake in that affirmation.

Gayatri Spivak has of course been most vociferous in her exploration of the problems and the possibilities of ethical representation. Influenced, inter alia, by critical theory and by Derrida's deconstructionism, Spivak's arguments have always attended to the question of representation where the textual and the political are entwined. The influence of her article 'Can the Subaltern Speak?' (1988) continues to be felt in feminist work on ethics as elsewhere; there, she opposed the idea that a subaltern group could be merely represented without a form of violence being done both to the heterogeneity of the group (and their interests) supposedly so named, nor without a certain disingenuousness in the forgetting of the role of colonialism played in producing the subaltern. Elsewhere she has explained that 'it is not a solution, the idea of the disenfranchised speaking for themselves, or the radical critics speaking for them, [because] this question of representation, self-representation, representing others, is a problem. On the other hand, we cannot put it under the carpet with demands for authentic voices; we have to remind ourselves that as we do this we might be compounding the problem even as we are trying to solve it' (1993: 63). What, she asks, is the possibility of generating a radical feminist politics that is responsive to others but without encouraging 'the metropolitan feminist' to ask 'all women to become like herself' in a world where economic development is mistaken for health and all relevant debates are approached as if they are (to be) structured just as they are in the 'Western world' (1998: 342). This leads to a reduction of the other to the same, so that for example, Western feminists consider their model of themselves as rights-bearing citizens as the future for women elsewhere.

Spivak's negotiations of the (im)possibility of maintaining an ethical relation with the singularity of the other have led her to consider a notion of ethical *translation* as a means of engagement that, as Sara Ahmed has noted, 'moves between distance and proximity' so that the necessity and dangers of the decisions made in the 'reading' are admitted and foregrounded (1998: 63). Ahmed herself has explored this aspect of Spivak's work in relation to her own consideration of the ethical possibilities of an unfetishized approach to 'the other' (2000). Spivak has also made the *pedagogic* a central concern, and the role of teaching has become a privileged site of ethical relations in her work. She has spoken, for example, about the possibilities of feminist teachers teaching (themselves and) their students not to hide behind the pretence of self-effacing gestures that remove their right to speak about and criticize things outside their immediate identity or experience. Educating oneself about the historical construction of one's own positionality and that of other people can earn one the right to speak and be heard respectfully, Spivak argues, and saying 'I can't speak about that' because of what one is (such as white, male or privileged) is another way of salving one's conscience in the name of political correctness (1993: 62).

As one can sense from the direction of much of this work, there is a certain necessity that the feminist critique of ethical theory should also place the feminist pursuit of ethics itself under question. For a start, because feminists have long been circling the argument that feelings of virtue are not always entirely innocently come by, not even in feminism, and 'being a good feminist' probably involves sentiments that are less than ethically pure. Likewise, it will be argued here that the relationship between 'ethics' and feminist politics has to be posed without resorting to the comfort of a formulation that sees feminism as simply the political expression of a feminist ethics.

To put the question baldly: Does feminist politics flow from an ethical disposition? The unhesitating response to this question must surely be affirmative. Feminist politics responds to the sufferings of women, and seeks to remedy those sufferings by rooting out injustices on every level. Without an element of ethical disposition, what would inspire feminist endeavours, pull feminism along and feminists together? And yet, is not the notion of an ethical feminism a utopian aspiration, an idealized assessment of the way feminist politics is conducted? Is the alternative formulation of feminist theory found in debate with a Nietzschean-inspired interlocutor who exposes feminism as an engagement that seeks not truth or justice, but power (an argument that Jane Flax made in reference to the debates around the threat that post-structuralist thought was seen to hold for feminism (Flax, 1993)) altogether more realistic? And if that is the case, are feminists, and feminist academics in particular, one suspects, obliged to accept an image of ourselves as fuelled by *ressentiment*, attached to our wounded identities[3] with the notion of women's sufferings posited as an excuse or else as a security blanket?

The writer who most boldly and provocatively explores these latter assertions is Wendy Brown (1995, 2001), who unflinchingly explores the possible underbelly of certain sentiments and fantasies deployed within radical politics. Feminism, as a form of identity politics, is considered here as *all* political. Brown writes:

> In its emergence as a protest against marginalisation and subordination, politicised identity thus becomes attached to its own exclusion both because it is premised on this exclusion for its very existence as identity and because the formation of identity at the site of exclusion, as exclusion, augments or 'alters the direction of suffering' entailed in subordination or marginalisation by finding a site of blame for it. (1995: 74)

But ultimately, Brown continues, this route that attempts to avenge a hurt 'reaffirms it, discursively codifies it' (1995: 74), such that it depends upon it and thereby curtails its political imagination, unable to hold out a future – for itself or for others – 'that triumphs over this pain' (1995: 74). In place of identity politics, Brown suggests a position that echoes that of Flax. She suggests that a language of 'wanting to be' or 'wanting to have' – a politics that refuses ontological claims in its adoption of a more expressly political language (1995: 76) – might shift identity politics from an 'angry spectatorship',[4] which trades in accusations of blame, toward more productive struggles in which futures can be imagined.

In this chapter, I wonder whether it is possible to take a middle route between these two positions and to argue that rather than seeking the cosiness and righteousness of some formulation of an ethical feminism, against which Elizabeth Spelman implicitly warns, and rather than giving up completely on ethics and feminism as a coupling, regarding identity politics as an impoverished and complicit reaction to power,[5] one might begin to formulate a position that takes as its point of departure a response to Levinas's ethics of non-(in)difference, takes a detour through Foucault, in order to build an argument that may seem, at first, counter-intuitive. I want to argue that to attempt to pursue something called 'ethical feminism' as if politics flowed from ethics is misguided, since the ethical can never be a basis or originary source for feminism. And while this refusal of an 'ethical feminism' as a goal is not due to a *failure* of feminism to be ethical exactly, the argument is that there is a hiatus between ethics and politics in so far as politics obliges one to engage in the non-ethical. Indeed, it is in the way that the dangers of the non-ethical are handled that politics begins, so that our focus as feminists may be more usefully trained on the temptations of the un-ethical than on the promises of the ethical. Accepting as much, one can turn again to the question of ethics figured neither as a source of politics nor as a political weapon, but as a check on freedom, an inspiration that prompts a continual questioning of one's own positionality, including, and here is the Foucauldian twist in the tale, the conditions of possibility of one's ethical sensibilities.

This argument only works, of course, if one agrees to the definitions of its terms, and I am already within Levinas's terms as I write these contentious statements. In the next section I introduce Levinas's writings on ethics, and outline the particular aspects of his writings and comments that I have found thought-provoking and troubling. Levinas's work concerns the question of ethics throughout, but here I am going to foreground one particular article, 'Useless Suffering' (1998a), because while it relies upon, and thereby enables me to introduce, his more general arguments, it also raises some stark and difficult points.

Levinas: The Ethical and the Non-ethical

Levinas insisted that the ethical relation actually structures subjectivity:

> I am defined as a subjectivity, as a singular person, as an 'I' precisely because I am exposed to the other. It is my inescapable and incontrovertible answerability to the other that makes me an individual 'I' to the extent that I agree to depose or dethrone myself – to abdicate my position of centrality – in favour of the vulnerable other. (in dialogue with Richard Kearney, 1986: 27)

Although Levinas did, on occasion, use the word 'love' to describe this relationship to the other in which the other is elevated and privileged (e.g. 1998a: 100), he also explains that he prefers other terms in which to speak about the responsibility that I have to the other. In 'Philosophy, Justice and Love' he describes it as taking upon oneself the *fate* of the other:

> From the start, the encounter with the Other is my responsibility for him. That is the responsibility for my neighbour, which is, no doubt, the harsh name for what we call love of one's neighbour; love without Eros, charity, love in which the ethical aspect dominates the passionate aspect, love without concupiscence. I don't very much like the word love, which is worn-out and debased. Let us speak instead of the taking upon oneself of the fate of the other. (1998b: 103)

The fate of the other is taken on not through decision, but through what Theodore de Boer calls the 'naivete of a direct impulse' that responds to the 'visage and visitation' of the other. It is a response to an accusation. In de Boer's interpretation, the absolute exteriority of the other, in which there is the trace of alterity (infinity, or God), unseats me, calling my freedom into question. The other makes freedom ashamed and limits its unlimitedness (1986: 93). Levinas says in conversation with Richard Kearney,

> in the relation to the face I am exposed as a usurper of the place of the other ... my duty to respond to the other suspends my natural right to self-survival, *le droit vitale*. My ethical relation of love for the other stems from the fact that the self cannot survive by itself alone, cannot find meaning within its own being-in-the-world, within the ontology of sameness. That is why I prefaced *Otherwise than Being or Beyond Essence* with Pascal's phrase 'That is my place in the sun.' That is how the usurpation of the whole world began. (1986: 24)

The freedom that one has to take the place of the other, to pursue one's own ends, is limited by the ethical relation, by the face of the other that says 'thou shalt not kill' forbidding the 'murderous nature of my natural will to put my own existence first' (Levinas, 1986: 24). Ethics is always first and foremost, in Levinas, a response to the other, but it is clear that ethics also relies upon my freedom and upon my response to the temptation of my own non-ethical, selfish, even murderous, impulses. It makes one aware that being is not its own reason for being:

> A truly human life cannot remain life satis-fied in its equality to being, a life of quietude, ... [instead] it is awakened by the other, that is to say, that being is never – contrary to what so many reassuring traditions say – its own reason for being. (1985: 122, emphasis in original)

Whenever one is awakened by the other, summoned by another's suffering, one cannot avoid being responsive. There is an appeal to which one is obliged to respond; one's freedom – the fact that there are several possible paths before one – is called into question and there begins the question of responsibility. One's very alterity, one's exteriority, is the only promise of salvation (1998a: 93) for the suffering other. Their suffering calls out; silently perhaps, or else with the involuntary noise that pain produces from the body-become-instrument as it momentarily turns outward even as its suffering pulls it excruciatingly inward. This is what Levinas terms the inter-human order, the appeal of one to the other. When pain does not 'eclipse the totality of the mental', 'a moan, a cry, a groan or a sigh slips through – the original call for aid, for curative help (1998a: 93).

The inter-human order is this moment of pure responsiveness, of non-indifference. And this response of non-indifference is pure because it is an altruism that exists prior to and is not conditioned by moral rules or by notions of reciprocity. Levinas wrote:

> The inter-human lies in a non-indifference of one to another in a responsibility of one for another but before the reciprocity of this responsibility, which will be inscribed in impersonal laws, comes to be superimposed on the pure altruism of this responsibility inscribed in the ethical position of the *I qua I*. (1998a: 100)

The ethical relation, therefore, is the asymmetrical moment before the banality of customs and the impersonal symmetrical form of laws. That is, before the other is dissolved into all others, and certainly before the other's response to me is under consideration.

It is important to emphasize the notion of asymmetry in Levinas's argument. In *Totality and Infinity* Levinas argued that ethics must maintain the necessary and difficult asymmetry, so that there is no dissolution of the unique moment of response, and the alterity of the other is maintained. Non-(in)difference holds open the difference between me and the other. The other is not the same as me, and nor can her exteriority be ignored by forms of interiorization or incorporation that would be forms of knowledge or power (possession). This is a crucial aspect of ethics for Levinas. He wrote,

> A calling into question of the same – which cannot occur within the egoist spontaneity of the same – is brought about by the other. We name this calling into question of my spontaneity by the presence of the Other ethics. The strangeness of the other, his irreducibility to the I, to my thoughts and my possessions, is precisely accomplished as a calling into question of my spontaneity, as ethics. (1969: 43)

In 'Useless Suffering' Levinas makes the relation to the other even more difficult by arguing that it is not only murder or usurping the place of the

suffering other – along with ontology that reduces the other to the same – that
are non-ethical paths in the face of the other's suffering, but so too is any
attempt to make a context for that suffering, and thus to give it meaning.
Suffering is meaningless, argues Levinas, it is for nothing (1998a: 93). But in
responding to another's suffering there is a temptation to give it meaning, to
provide some sort of context for it. This temptation to give meaning to
another's suffering Levinas warns against, because here again is the temptation
to the non-ethical. Why?

Witnessing or even having knowledge of another's suffering is a form of
incorporation. We take it in. Although this taking in may express itself through
bodily sensations or movements, it is not suffering in oneself. Its exteriority
cannot be interiorized. Levinas's argument in 'Useless Suffering' is that one's
response to suffering in others cannot be an attempt to share that suffering as
if one were able to experience that same suffering. Nor can it be a further form
of incorporation, which would be to provide a contextualization that understands that suffering in terms of a higher and ultimate purpose. If our response
to the suffering of this century – he speaks here especially of the suffering
caused by Hitler's National Socialism – takes a form of comprehending it as
part of some ultimate good, a good perhaps incomprehensible to us in the
present time, then the response becomes a mode of contextualization which is
a mode of justification of suffering. Therein lies 'the source of all immorality'
argues Levinas; to justify another's suffering (1998a: 99). These remarks were
aimed at particular forms of religious comprehension, and this response leads
to Levinas's argument that Western thought's theodicy has come to an end.
After theodicy, one is left, argues Levinas, with a more difficult form of faith,
one that does not have the consolation of a greater plan, but one that positions
the *I* as a compassionate *I*, so that suffering takes on a meaning as suffering *for*
the other, and can only then become a non-useless suffering.

The challenge is to be able to respond without totalizing forms of incorporation that deny the alterity of the other, making the other the same as oneself,
or making her part of an already written story. Levinas's ethics relies upon
maintaining the alterity of the other, so that the asymmetry between one and
the other is not collapsed into the same, into identification, as if I could share
her suffering. The possibility of identification is refused, while the suffering
that the suffering of the other produces in me, is the only meaning that suffering can have. This is the complexity of what Levinas calls *non-(in)difference*;
how to hold open the distance of difference while making the other proximate
and responding to her useless suffering by allowing it to take on some meaning
through my compassionate response.

Feminism: Between Ethics and Politics?

Clearly Levinas is not thinking about ethics as a form of critique of political movements such as feminism; his focus is principally a critique of ontology and theodicy, with the spectre of National Socialism not far from his mind. His engagement with feminism was negligible, and interest in the question of sexual difference was troubling, minimal and frequently deferred (see Chanter, 1995). Nevertheless, in this section I want to employ those aspects of his philosophy outlined above in order to follow through the suggestion that arguing for the refinement of an ethical feminism is a misguided endeavour. It is not that feminism cannot be regarded as an ethical enterprise, but such an attempt requires that ethics be understood as somehow gathered into political strategies. But the ethical response to the other cannot be so gathered, for to do so is to force the singularity of the response to the other into a generalized formulation. Better, I wish to suggest, to regard feminism as entailing a political negotiation of the necessarily non-ethical.

It is difficult, following Levinas's definitions, not to see feminism as engaged in manoeuvres, both philosophical and political, that make symmetrical the relation between me and the other, creating a sameness out of difference, and interiorizing the exteriority of the other through modes of incorporation. Indeed, feminism has drawn power from its history of identifications between women and the rhetoric, at least, of shared sufferings. Feminist theory could be regarded as a totalizing incorporation that borders on theodicy in that it seeks to comprehend women's sufferings, explaining them through its terms, and attempting to give them meaning in the sense that the incorporation of sufferings within its political aspirations could lead to their alleviation in some imagined future. Moreover, feminism has, by definition, its exclusionary aspects in that its responsibility is not to the other, any other, but to particular others[6] – women – whose particularity defines and 'trains' the feminist response.

These points do not need to be laboured, because although reading them through Levinas may put a different spin on them, these dangers are ones that feminism has been aware of for some time, and they have been discussed and debated without the aid of an excursion through Levinas's writing, albeit in different terms and with different inflections. Numerous feminist writers have discussed these aspects of feminist politics in many different frameworks. Most of these discussions, however, have sought to remedy the situation by *improving* the way we conceive feminist politics and its subject. Thus, for example, Julia Kristeva's 'Women's Time' lent her approval to a feminism that would leave behind the religious overtures of what she regarded as second wave feminism in order to reach a third wave where the centrality of the distinction between man and woman would be interrogated as an unstable, metaphysical category.

Bonnie Honig argued that feminists could adopt a strategy from Hannah Arendt's politics of performative production in order to 'unmask, subvert, and resist the violent closures of the univocity and self-evidence assumed by some Jewish and feminist politics of identity?' (1992: 231). Drucilla Cornell, who acknowledges a debt to Levinas's ethics of the other, argued in 'What is Ethical Feminism?' that:

> this call to responsibility [from 'women of color, lesbians, and others designated as outside the matrix of heterosexuality'] inheres in the aspiration to the ethical relationship and is as a result a crucial aspect of what I call ethical feminism ... it demands of us that we deconstruct the claim that there is an identity that we share as women and that the differences between us are secondary. (1995: 85)

The desire of feminist theory and politics has been to put right these aspects of feminism that make symmetrical, that totalize or theologize, and make feminism, if you will, *more ethical*.

In contrast, I want to focus on the tension between feminism as a political endeavour – that, indeed, seeks power and is motivated by a desire to achieve change – and feminist response as an ethical responsivity. My suggestion is to use Levinas in a challenging way, to ask what would result were one to approach the question of ethics and feminism not as the question 'what is an ethical feminism?' or 'how can feminism become more ethical?', but if instead one asked the question 'how does feminism negotiate the necessary tension between ethics and politics?' How can feminists attempt the compassionate complexities of non-(in)difference where the ethical moment is not diminished within feminist analyses and strategies?

In Levinas, the move from ethics to politics is not understood as the former informing the latter. There is a hiatus there that seemingly cannot be bridged (Critchley, 1999). As I have outlined above, the ethical relation stems from the other, whose singularity calls on my singularity in the inter-human. But political change for Levinas is not on the level of the inter-human in this way. Ethics 'cannot legislate for society or produce rules of conduct whereby society might be revolutionized or transformed. It does not operate on the level of the manifesto *or call to order*; it is not a *savoir vivre*' (Levinas with Kearney, 1986: 29, emphasis in original). As soon as one is in the situation of responding to the other, of deciding to respond and how to respond, the ethical, as infinite response to the other, is left behind. Some have argued, with Derrida, that the decision is a moment of madness, choosing to respond to this person, to this suffering and in this way, is no longer a question of ethics but of interestedness (see Critchley, 1999 on Derrida). The response is *interested* in the sense that there is an attempt to effect change. Ethics, by contrast, is 'dis-inter-ested' for Levinas because it

precedes our interest in being, our *inter-est*, as a being-in-the-world attached to property and appropriating what is other than itself to itself. Morality is what governs the
world of political 'inter-estedness', the social interchanges between citizens in a
society. Ethics, as the extreme exposure and sensitivity of one subjectivity to another,
becomes morality and hardens its skin as soon as we move into the political world of
the third – the world of government, institutions, tribunals, prisons, schools, commit-
tees, and so on. (Levinas 1986: 29–30)

Thus for Levinas, it seems, ethics involves a response of one to one other;
politics necessarily involves the appearance of the third, and embroils one in
the question of choosing between cases and of judgement. Ethics is passive in
its responsibility;[7] politics is active. It seems more realistic to accept feminism
as a political endeavour that involves a negotiation of the break with ethics
since, in the political, interested, concerns of feminism there is of necessity the
temptation to totalize in one form of incorporation or another, that is, to
understand, to attempt to share, or to contextualize gender inequalities and
women's sufferings. In the name of effecting change, of being political, the
other's particularity and exteriority is diminished and interiorized.
Furthermore, there is always *another* other who appears, who challenges the
privileging we may be giving to one woman or set of women, to one issue
rather than another. An ethical response to the other is always questioned by
the appearance of that other other. Rather than see this as a situation that can
be avoided by 'getting better' at feminism, or improving the ethical foundation
of our politics, one can accept that these negotiations are part and parcel of
political argument, feminist included. Indeed, one might argue with Critchley,
who argues with Derrida, that 'if there is to be no deduction from ethics to politics, then this can be both ethically and politically welcome' (1999: 275).

However, rather than the conclusion that there is no place for the ethical
within feminism, which might posit feminism as *all* politics and all politics as
either machination or a series of singular decisions, with ethics figured as prior
to and always eclipsed by the political, I would like to suggest here that there
is the possibility of incorporating ethics within a conception of the political
that takes up Levinas's challenge in a particular way. This asks again about the
role of ethics within the political.

In a most compelling analysis, Ewa Ziarek in her *Ethics of Dissensus:
Postmodernity, Feminism and the Politics of Radical Democracy* (2001), also
explores the implications of the thought of Levinas in a feminist and post-structuralist context. Of most relevance here is Ziarek's critique of the reading of
Levinas that would understand the finite nature of politics as continually inter-
rupted by the infinity of the ethical. Finding another description of radical politics, she suggests that the relation between ethics and politics can be
complicated and reformulated. Levinas himself warned against a comprehension of political justice as 'a degradation of the for-the-other, a diminution, a

limitation of anarchic responsibility' (1981: 159), she points out. Furthermore, in *Totality and Infinity* Levinas implies that the question of political justice is not merely superimposed or added to the asymmetrical relation to the Other, since the ethical subject is from the start answerable to all others: the epiphany of the face in and of itself 'opens humanity' (2001: 65). Ziarek argues that the 'responsibility for the Other always already bears a relation to all others' (2001: 66) precisely because alterity is not just 'infinitely transcendent' and 'infinitely foreign' but is *also* both comparable and immanent. In this way Ziarek contests those who render ethics outside the political frame, by suggesting that the asymmetrical relation to the Other straight away opens the question of politics, while additionally, the proliferation of differences within democratic politics 'retains a reference to anarchic responsibility' (2001: 66).

A not unrelated way to read Levinas is to see that there is, despite the emphasis on hiatus, a relationship between ethics and politics, since 'the norm that must continue to inspire and direct the moral order is the ethical norm of the interhuman' (Levinas 1986: 30). It is necessary to accept the presence of the state and its institutions, to live in the world of citizens as well as in the order of the face to face, argued Levinas, but 'it is in terms of the relation to the Face or of me before the other that we can speak about the legitimacy or illegitimacy of the state' (1998b: 107). In this way Levinas intimated that people will test and contest the form of state against the extent to which ethical practices are permitted. So although his ethical philosophy is explicitly not intended to *prescribe* personal behaviours let alone political behaviours, there is a sense that political forms are put to test – are checked – on the level of the ethical, as a site of both inspiration and freedom. The advantage of such a perspective over other versions of democratic politics is that, like Ziarek's notion of an 'ethics of dissensus', it guards against a version of politics that could absolutely contain or express ethics. For democratic politics can all too easily translate questions of ethics into a language of calculation and exchange (cf. Ziarek 2001: 67) staging a competition that rules out of contention the state and its regulations. Ziarek brilliantly ties this point to Patricia Williams's arguments in *The Alchemy of Race and Rights* (1991) who in her discussion of human rights argued that while rights have the potential to elevate one's status from human body to social being (1991: 153), their use had also to be understood historically and relationally. The 'dry process of reification' of rights, wrote Williams, had to be tempered with 'a larger definition of privacy and property: so that privacy is turned from exclusion based on self-regard into regard for another's fragile autonomy' (1991: 164). For Levinas, argues Ziarek, and so too for her 'ethics of dissensus', human rights are not expressed in the laws, but are the premise on which laws and legality are to be interrogated (2001: 69).

One might conclude, then, that feminist politics is not caused, does not *arise* from ethics; but that ethics occupies exactly this role of checking its politics.

The inter-human in Levinas's terms, or Williams's 'fragile autonomy', accompanies political articulations and endeavours. The expansiveness of the ethical is entwined with the politics of feminism, seeking expression there, but in a double gesture, standing aside from it, interrogating it. Indeed, much feminist politics has been exemplary in this respect in so far as feminism has engaged in a reflexive questioning of its political rhetoric and strategies in relation to its non-ethical tendencies. If ethics is in the sensation that Levinas calls shame – one might name it other things too – which descends upon one wherever one is taking someone else's place, or else eclipsing, incorporating, or forgetting another, and if it arises wherever one becomes aware that there are many paths to choose from, that one's choices mean leaving some of those paths untaken and unconsidered, then these are surely the questions that have occupied much feminist thought. Some of the most bitterly contested debates within feminism have been less about political strategy and more about the ethical question, if you will, of the other. Whose suffering is being diminished, eclipsed, excluded? Who is being reduced to and incorporated as the same? Any contemporary discussion of feminist ethics would have these issues centre-stage. In such discussions, feminisms' ethical disposition is put into question. The spontaneity of feminist analysis, categories and thought is checked.

Conditions of Possibility

But such a conclusion is only momentarily satisfying, for while a commitment to be open to the interrogation of 'the ethical' cannot be all bad, and might lead to a reflexive feminist practice, alongside these issues another set of questions, the most difficult questions, needs to be voiced. And here we reach perhaps the limits of Levinas's usefulness in this discussion. What I mean to suggest at this point is that the relationship between ethics and politics in Levinasian terms does not take one to perhaps the most challenging issues, which to my mind are those that concern *conditions of possibility*. When the hiatus between ethics and politics is defined as a move from the face-to-face relation to the third, to justice and judgement, one removes the question of the political constitution and contestation of ethical response in the sense that the little matter of asking 'what constitutes suffering?' 'how does one recognize suffering?' may deal the logic of the discussion thus far a crashing blow.

Feminists know well the political nature of the endeavour to contest definitions of suffering and injustice. In the history of feminist arguments, it is clear that the case for a gendered form of suffering has frequently had to be made. That is, when suffering is not apparent, when suffering is understood as natural or deserved, when an injustice is perhaps unknown to its victim, when there is even an element of enjoyment in some inequity, the case for regarding this *as* suffering and *responding* to suffering has to be made; people have to be persuaded and political interpretations and understandings of the world are all important in the demands and arguments that ensue. William Connolly has made a similar point in his discussion of ethics:

> some of the most difficult cases [in ethics] arise when people suffer from injuries imposed by institutionalised identities, principles and cultural understandings, when those who suffer are not entirely helpless but are defined as threatening, contagious, or dangerous to the self-assurance of these identities, and when the sufferers honor sources of ethics inconsonant or disturbing to these constituencies. (1999: 129)

More difficult still is the fact that, in the questioning of conditions of possibility, it becomes incumbent upon one to ask the same questions of one's own ethical sensibilities: how have I been constituted as an arbiter of suffering, as one able to recognize suffering? How one understands what suffering is, how one responds to suffering, how one's ethical responses are trained – socially, historically, culturally – even before any political strategy or proposed solutions to a particular instance or issue are on the agenda – are crucial, and already *political* questions. Genealogical investigations operate exactly here, disrupting the comfort of any formulation whereby ethics is viewed as a question of response to suffering. Long ago, Nietzsche's *Genealogy of Morals* drew attention to the murky undercurrents of ideals of good, linking the very distinction between good and evil to the anticipated pleasure in being able to categorize and punish evil in the name of good (1967/1887: 65–7); feelings of shame, for Nietzsche, would never be a true foundation for ethical behaviour, since shame and guilt were only to be understood as sentiments resulting from the internalization processes by which humans were constituted by Christian morality. Nietzsche's polemic was directed at prompting people to ask questions of their taken-for-granted values, not because these values were wrong and need to be righted, but because their sedimentation limited people's ability to think differently.

> It goes without saying that I do not deny – unless I am a fool – that many actions called immoral ought to be avoided and resisted, or that many called moral ought to be done and encouraged – but I think that one should be encouraged and the other avoided *for other reasons than hitherto*. We have to *learn to think differently* – in order at last, perhaps very late on, to attain even more: *to feel differently*. (Nietzsche 1982: 104, emphasis in original)

Feeling differently however, cannot be legislated for. One can only hope that through genealogical investigation there may be a different perspective learnt, a view from 'from afar', that makes our most precious values, thoughts and ideas, appear strange. That would be a successful genealogical investigation. It doesn't necessarily mean those values and views would change; but it does offer the possibility of prompting different modes of thought and with them different modes of feeling.

Foucault's genealogical researches were fuelled by a sense of curiosity in the sense that, as he once remarked, 'the word ... evokes concern: it evokes the care one takes for what exists and what could exist; a readiness to find strange and singular what surrounds us; a certain relentlessness to break up our familiarities and to regard otherwise the same things' (1996: 305). Many of Foucault's later works were detailed analyses focused around the question: how has it been possible to be recognized as an as ethical subject? His purpose in these investigations was to provide genealogical appreciation of the present, to show how the way we regard certain actions and their relation to ethics have altered over time. The later volumes of the *History of Sexuality* continued Foucault's interest in the history of problematization, the way that things come to be regarded as problems (see Foucault 1996: 414). In Foucault's genealogical investigations, therefore, the passivity that Levinas accords to ethical disposition is scrutinized; there is inserted between one and the other the complex web of ethical codes that pertain to one's specific historical, social and cultural conjuncture.

Regarding ethical sensibilities, including the sensation of shame, as contingent and produced is a stance that is feared by some, and with good reason since it is true that such a stance can be articulated as part of an apathy toward both ethical and political questions. Moreover, it can be used in a way that returns the focus of discussion away from the other to the self (Smart, 1998), or to a remote history. The task, therefore, is to use such investigations to prompt questions both about the self and about the other. How have I been produced as a subject who cares for others? What are the conditions and the limits of my care for others? How has the moment in which I become ashamed of my freedom and am prompted to think and feel differently been constituted for me? How have the moments in which I do not?

Indeed, it could be argued that there is a core concern in genealogical work, which is precisely the question of the other, in the sense that genealogies pursue historical trajectories of certain truths in order to consider the contingency of the self and therefore to promote regard for the other that *one might have been*. The purpose of doing so, I would argue, is not only in the familiar sense that one thinks oneself into the shoes of another – that one has some sense of how the other whom one despises, fears, ignores, surpasses, judges, pathologizes *could have been me* – but that one thinks about the contingency of the very processes by which I feel fear, indifference, hatred, superiority and so on. These responses are rendered contingent because the lines that demarcate the difference of me from the other, and the sentiments and the knowledge by which one recognizes the quality of the relation of difference between myself and the other, are rendered contingent.[8] Thus one is returned to Connolly's description of genealogy, which emphasizes the aspect of display – of displaying the 'intelligible' against a newly imagined background – of emptiness, or (only seemingly conversely) of all possible spaces.

The ethical sensibility that arises then from genealogy would be one that further radicalizes Levinas's ethics of non-indifference, because the passivity of the relation to the other is met with the scrutiny of genealogical enquiry. One cannot simply rely upon oneself to respond to the call, or command, of the other, but in addition, one must respond to one's own response, including non-response, both in Levinasian terms, according to its potentially totalizing tendencies, and in Foucauldian terms, genealogically. Along with an ethics of welcoming, of listening to the other, of allowing the other's suffering to reverberate without being incorporated, one has an ethics of self-interrogation. One becomes attuned to the probability that the conditions of possibility of one's ethical response mean that there are *unforeseen* totalizing, diminishing or excluding tendencies, unanticipated and which we may not be able to articulate as yet. Thus we arrive at a doubling moment in which one's ethically disposed subjectivity must also become the object of one's genealogical scrutiny; and this without losing the sense of the irreducibility of the other. Ethics is exhausting, and never exhausted. Infinite responsibility.

To return to my question: how is feminism to negotiate the necessary tension between ethics and politics? One can now think about giving this a fuller answer. First, one is obliged to accept that in the terms set out here, political arguments exceed or leave behind ethical response, so that feminist politics, as all others, results from decisions that involve a negotiation of the non-ethical. Secondly, although ethics cannot be regarded as the basis or cause of politics, it can operate as an 'inspiration' and check for politics, by asking how open is the possibility of response and responsibility, and how attentive to the other the political culture, and one's politics within it, enables one to be. Thirdly, ethical responses, while coming from the Other, have also to be subjected to genealogical critique, since the constitution of ethical response involves questions that are political and that are bound up with the lines of difference across which identity and so much morality is constructed. And fourthly, in each of these three points there are complex manoeuvres with respect to the self, who is both passive but always active in relation to that passivity.

Much feminist debate is I believe embroiled in finding pathways out of the complexities of compassionate non-indifference. The scrutiny under which 'the feminist subject' has been placed has been considerable. I believe that this scrutiny is an important part of feminist struggle, and that the moments when feminism almost seems to dissolve itself in debate are testimony to the rigours by which feminists are willing to challenge their ethical and their political constitution. Rather than be concerned to develop an ethical feminism that regards feminism as an ethical project, and that attempts to still the tensions and complexities of the relationship between ethics and politics by making one cause or encompass the other, I believe that it is only in the attentiveness to their relations that we find any hope. It is within these theoretical concerns, therefore, that a notion of performativity can be carefully linked to debates and discussion about ethics and politics. Again, the course of my journey runs close to that of Ewa Ziarek, who reminds us that Derrida (1982) has spoken of the declaration of rights as precisely performative, depending 'not only on the preservation of law but also on the force of rupture separating the new formulation from its original legal context' (Ziarek 2001: 70); the performative declaration of rights by a disenfranchised group refers to existing law, in other words, but it expresses and holds open the possibility of future breaks with legality. There is maintained, therefore, 'some irruptive violence' (Derrida 1990: 27). As in the radical democracy that Ziarek imagines, therefore, to comprehend political interventions less as expressions of ethical sentiment than as performative interventions with a complex relationship to 'the ethical' is also to understand performativity as an opening onto the future. If for Levinas this is the messianic, irreducible, utopian element, and for Williams, as Ziarek points out, it is a 'moral utopianism', 'a fiercely motivational, almost religious, source of hope' (Williams 1991: 163), it is for Ziarek herself 'an inscription of the diachrony of responsibility into the futural politics of human rights [preserving] a noncoincidence at the core of democracy' (Williams 1991: 72). In other words, democracy rests upon the plurality of definitions of justice. Ziarek finds her optimism then in the sense that despite its track record the structure of democracy is such that in a sense it allows a future in which its bases are questioned.

The potential violence of the performative is precisely what returns us to the conclusions drawn above from the Levinasian notion of the non-ethical. Derrida famously drew attention to this aspect of Levinas's work – 'Language can only indefinitely tend toward justice by acknowledging and practicing violence within it. Violence against violence' (1978: 117) – such that one cannot be complacent about formulations of the relationship between ethics and politics. As I have argued here, as soon as 'the ethical' becomes 'the political' it is embroiled in the negotiation of the non-ethical.[9] To argue the performativity of political claims, therefore, is less a call for celebration than a caution that, while radical politics is an expression of the futural nature of democratic political structures, the justice claims, which it in some sense invites, need always to be accompanied by the interrogations of the identities and sentiments there performed.

Such a stance has its critics, of course, not least those who object that in emphasizing the importance of genealogical critique as a necessary accompaniment to an openness to the asymmetry of the Other, there is a tendency to encourage the political subject into an endless navel-gazing, applauding procrastinations that ultimately render her *a*political. In the next chapter (Chapter 4), I will attend to an extreme although proximate instance of such a critique, one that has explicitly argued that feminist politics – indeed all politics – is threatened by such a stance. In the following chapter (Chapter 5), I will explore a different set of questions concerning the politics of genealogy and suggest that the challenges there are ones that have more searching implications on the level of theory, ethics and politics within feminism and beyond. These I will take up in Chapter 6.

CHAPTER 4

Rhetorical Figures: On 'Dangerous Thought', Fear and Politics

What we commonly call nihilism – and are tempted to date historically, decry politically, and ascribe to thinkers who allegedly dared to think 'dangerous thoughts' – is
actually a danger inherent in the thinking activity itself. There are no dangerous
thoughts; thinking itself is dangerous, but nihilism is not its product.

Arendt, 'Thinking and Moral Considerations'

With Arendt, one might reasonably argue that nihilism is not the result of
thinking in a certain way, but is a necessary part of the process of thinking
itself, in the sense that whenever one is truly thinking, one is involved in the
suspension of certainties in order to lessen the hold that concepts, norms and
morals have over one's thought habits and patterns. Thus Arendt argued that
to be thinking is to 'stop everything else, and this everything else, again whatever it may happen to be, interrupts the thinking process; it is *as though we were
moved to another world*' (1984: 13, italics added). In this 'other world' of
thought, objects are necessarily absent; or, rather, they are present only as representations in the mind of the thinker. As Aristotle understood, Arendt argues
in a footnote, the mind has the ability to make present what is absent; the mind
can handle absences through its deployment of imagination and remembrance
(and even 'beyond the realm of all possible imagination' (1984: 14), that is,
beyond the use of images and representation, since via the use of reason the
mind can, for example, think infinity).

Understood as such, thinking is an internal conversation with figures of the
imagination, with absences; it has itself no result since it has no *appearance*,
and cannot therefore be judged dangerous or otherwise. And because it has no
result in and of itself, the relevance of thinking in relation to the world can only
be investigated by beginning with the activity itself as an experience:

How can anything relevant for the world we live in arise out of so resultless an enterprise? An answer, if at all, can come only from the thinking activity, the performance
itself, which means that we have to trace experiences rather than doctrines. (1984: 16)

As Arendt develops her argument – an explicit reflection on Eichmann's buffoon-like lack of thinking, and read by some as an apologia for Heidegger – the performance/experience of thinking is described as a form of 'intercourse with oneself' (1984: 36) whose principle activity is the dissolution of one's own axioms, a notion she hears first in Kant's 'Introduction to Metaphysics' (1984: 15) and then elaborates in relation to Socrates. For Arendt, thinking is full of anti-fascist promise.

However, at the moment when thoughts are communicated in whatever form – through action, depiction, written or spoken word – it is clear that one has moved back from that 'other world' into this world of appearances. Furthermore, it is clear that one can begin to speak of the consequences and causes of thoughts or ways of thinking, and to argue and debate as to whether these communicated thoughts have the potential to do harm. In other words, it is only when thoughts become heard, and especially when they become 'public', and have the potential to circulate, that talk of dangerousness makes any sense. For in the move from thought-experiment to public statement, one has moved from internal assessment concerning one's own appreciation of a way of thinking, the tos and fros of internal 'perplexity' (as Socrates described his experience of thought, as well as the experience he hoped to induce in others, Arendt, 1984: 22) to making truth claims, or let us say, assertions in specific spaces.

Socrates saw his task, argues Arendt, as facilitating. He sought to wrest thought from 'opinion', to be the midwife delivering to others the possibility and freedom of reflection. But public assertions reach out to others in numerous ways, seeking not only to facilitate but also, perhaps above all, to persuade. That is, as soon as a thought-experiment becomes public, it becomes a form of communication. And, as such, it becomes an attempt to engage another's imagination. This is to say that we are also inevitably dealing with the modes of presentation of thoughts with all the pitfalls that 'conditions of hearing' entail. Any intervention will be received and debated by situated hearers within situated contexts.

The point is twofold: first, that although talk of 'dangerous thought' is strictly (Arendtianly) speaking nonsensical, it is perfectly acceptable for the question of 'dangerousness' to be posed at the point at which thought becomes communication, for example, in public speeches or published works. Secondly, that once there is further public comment on this 'public' form of thought, the question of the contexts of its reception (broadly construed) and, as this chapter will suggest, attention to the rhetoric by which it is presented and received become all-important to any analysis of the ensuing debate. The chapter will argue, furthermore, that attention to this latter point concerning reception must reintroduce aspects of that which occurs in Arendt's description of thinking. In particular, it suggests that rhetoric trades in figures of the imagination, in conjuring (up and with) spectres, and more importantly still, by performing their co-joining.[1] And in so far as this is true, there is always the possibility that one can be a poor Socrates – by error or by design – and, rather than facilitate thinking in one's audience, can use the opportunity for communication to close thought down or else to train it to one's line of argument.

Treating political assertions as processes of rhetorical 'cutting' whereby political speech and imagery attempt to direct and appeal to affectivities and to align subjectivities, this chapter argues that political processes rely crucially upon the drawing of rhetorical figures – here, especially of fear – such that one might argue that political exchange enacts a form of mimetic invention, an invention that draws upon cultural imagery for its power. The analysis of rhetorical figures deployed therein enable an understanding of how debate is animated and how enunciative positions are crafted and deployed.

The Rhetoric of Dangerousness and the Figure of Fascism

Michael Berube recalls a moment in his public debate with Alan Sokal in which a member of the audience 'went so far as to insist to me, in the question/answer session after Sokal and I had made our remarks that the left must entertain the possibility that there are moral imperatives the content of which we do not yet know, for to believe anything else is to open the door to fascism' (2000: 149). My argument here is that wherever a feminist argument or intervention *ends* with the charge 'that's dangerous, collaborative, evil, fascistic', of which there have been many instances in print, some of which I discussed in *Feminist Imagination* (1999) (and no doubt there have been many more off the page), there may be a failure to take this implicit frame of reference seriously enough. In particular, it seems to me that there might be some profound lessons to be drawn from pressing this point somewhat further, that is, in thinking about feminist theory in light of the changing political horizons that were the twentieth century. For while it is not news that feminist theory has been obliged to revise its faith in the practice of democracy, and nor is it news that feminist theorists might have to speak about racism as they speak about inequalities of gender, it seems to me that there is still space for thinking about these arguments as incumbent upon feminists *because* feminism itself flourished within the twentieth century and is in that sense *of* the twentieth century, with all its freedoms and all its horrors. These issues are, if sometimes only implicitly, *already* part of the feminist political landscape, and are referenced by the very concepts and modes of argument that feminists employ. Moreover, they are silently referenced in the *fears* of feminists.

The notion that some ways of thinking are dangerous will be familiar to readers of Euro-American philosophical and feminist-theoretical debates. What would it mean to approach these assertions of 'dangerous' anew, not as battles between theorists of different epistemological schools, but as situated forms of rhetoric, situated, that is, in relation to their historical conditions of possibility? If 'dangerousness' cannot be inherent in certain thoughts, how is it possible to cast it precisely as such?

Consider Martha Nussbaum's now notorious essay which reviewed Judith Butler's books and which was published in February 1999 in *The New Republic*. In the review essay of four of Butler's books, Nussbaum makes a number of charges against her work. First, that it is lofty, with an absence of any focus on women's lives or proposals as to how to bring about social change. Secondly, that her writing is exasperating to the extent that it verges on mystification. Thirdly, that her arguments are not especially new, but rather 'shopworn' notions clothed in an obscure style that makes them seem important; as such the work is not truly philosophy but closer to the 'manipulative methods' of sophistry and rhetoric. Fourthly, that since Butler gives few explanations and definitions of the philosophers she draws upon, but deals with abstract theory rather than material solutions, she can only be imagining her audience as a group of young and docile feminist scholars who ask no questions. Fifthly, Nussbaum makes some critiques of Butler's arguments, questioning for example some of the detail of her use of Austin and her allegiance to the Nietzschean perspective where 'there is no doer behind the deed'; she is also unconvinced that sex difference can be completely 'written off as culture'. But above all it is the implications for resistance that rile Nussbaum. She argues that if, as Butler implies, gender can be resisted by subversive and parodic acts, one has to have a means to understand which subversive acts are good and which are not; that is, one needs a normative theory of social justice.

It is this last point that moves Nussbaum to argue that Butler's work is dangerous. She writes:

> there is a void, then, at the heart of Butler's notion of politics. This void can look liberating, because the reader fills it implicitly with a normative theory of human equality or dignity. But let there be no mistake: for Butler, as for Foucault, subversion is subversion and it can in principle go in any direction. Indeed Butler's naively empty politics is *especially dangerous* for the very causes she holds dear. For every friend of Butler, eager to engage in subversive performances that proclaim the repressiveness of heterosexual gender norms, there are dozens who would like to engage in subversive performances that flout the norms of tax compliance, of non-discrimination, of decent treatment of one's fellow students. To such people we should say, you cannot merely resist as you please, for there are norms of fairness, decency, dignity that entail that this is bad behaviour. We have to articulate those norms – and this Butler refuses to do. (1999, emphasis added)

Moreover, for a woman for dislikes rhetoric, Martha Nussbaum ends her critique of Judith Butler with a stinging rhetorical flourish:

Judith Butler's hip quietism is a comprehensible response to the difficulty of realizing justice in America. But it is a bad response. It collaborates with evil. Feminism deserves more and women deserve better. (1999)

Some time after reading Nussbaum's essay, I received an article to review that, turning the tables on Nussbaum, compared her mode of argumentation with Jörg Haider of Austria's far-right Freedom Party. In this (anonymous) author's hands, it was she, with her certainties about what feminism should look like, who was cast as the dangerous thinker, compared point by point with the contemporary political programme of the Freedom Party, widely understood as fascistic. This manoeuvre illustrated just how differently one can position the target of one's critique, just how dependent the judgement of those receiving is on the contexts against which it is read, so much so that those who are understood as leading feminist theorists can be read as dangerous collaborators with evil, and those who defend normative theories of social justice can be read as fascistic.

Moments such as this are intriguing. What is the place of such provocative vocabulary and such startling frames of reference within the context of feminist debate? Certainly Nussbaum's critique of Butler is not isolated in this respect. For the record, I think both arguments, Nussbaum's and those articulated by the anonymous author, misrepresent their 'targets', but to detail my disagreements would be a different sort of intervention on my part. A more oblique and to my mind much more interesting line of questioning would start elsewhere, and would approach the debate as I have indicated, that is, as a moment in which contexts of reception and rhetorical manoeuvres are all important. To a large extent the debate is already 'about' rhetoric, for, despite her distaste for it, Nussbaum is just as concerned that Butler is not a *good enough* rhetorician as she is that Butler is *merely* a rhetorician. Many of her charges amount to the fact that Butler is not a good communicator, that her use of language is too obscure and abstract to be of use in furthering the feminist cause because it will not aid in the formation of 'un-ironic, organized public action'. She is concerned furthermore about the mode of reception of Butler's arguments since they could be deployed as justifications for non-egalitarian practices as much as egalitarian.

Here my interest in rhetoric is akin to that articulated by Stanley Fish when he argues that to pay attention to the products of rhetoric is to conceive that notion not as ephemeral, but 'as the medium in which certainties become established, in which formidable traditions emerge, are solidified, and become obstacles' (in Olsen, 2002: 95). It is heightened all the more in relation to this particular example by the few terms and arguments that raise the temperature of the debate by placing it within a specific historical context where specific political and cultural images are conjured up. What does the use of these

highly inflammatory terms – evil, fascistic – suggest about the imagined political context within which this disagreement is placed? Why does the strongest
possible manoeuvre one can make in forming an argument against another
feminist seem to be to place her thought in proximity with fascism, either
explicitly or else by casting her thinking as dangerous in such a way that it is
positioned as implicitly leaving the door open to extreme anti-democratic and
non-egalitarian politics, in other words, to totalitarianism? Moreover, what
intrigues me is the way that these questions are haunted in turn by a figure:
the evil or totalitarian interloper.

Now the contention that some post-structuralist refashionings of the project
of feminist theory are *dangerous* has become a familiar line of argument,
focusing especially on the reservation of judgement that results from the 'norm-
lessness' of post-structuralism. The worry is that feminist theory is left rudder-
less if it does not allow itself an appeal to foundations or to norms, a worry often
combined with a melancholic attitude that regrets and seeks to rectify the fissile
nature of contemporary feminist thought. Similar to those debates that linked
Nietzsche's questioning of morality to National Socialism's selective appeal to
his thought, this argument suggests that to think with him of good and evil as
having a history, of morality as a symptom (1967/1887: 20), or of gender as a
fragile and repeated 'fiction' takes away a foundation from which to argue or a
normative good to both appeal to and protect. How, the question runs, can we
follow feminist aspirations when our feminist philosophers are producing texts
that refuse to state what we want to see instated the world over, even in the
most basic terms such as freedom and equality? The very terms of Nussbaum's
critique, in which Butler's strategy of subversion could go in 'any direction',
where the latter is taken to task for being naive, and her theories as dangerous,
are remarkable, addressed as they are to the work of a woman who the writer
knows to 'hold dear' the same egalitarian values as she does herself. But the
argument that post-structuralist theory is dangerous frequently repeats this line
of argument; it is, furthermore, often concerned with what an author doesn't
say, with the absence of either clear foundational beliefs, norms or manifesto-
like demands and aspirations that might shore up theory and insulate it from an
imagined interloper. And it is exactly this fear that certain modes of argumentation have no armour to protect from the counter-claims of an undesirable
figure or movement that seems to usher in the spectre of totalitarianism, or
more specifically, of fascism. It is by highlighting this figure of the fascist interloper that I want to shift the focus away from the 'rights and wrongs' of Butler
or of post-structuralism and concentrate instead on noticing these rhetorical
processes whereby certain figures, stories and historico-political moments are
recalled and deployed as techniques of persuasion.

In *Feminist Imagination* one of my responses to these kinds of rhetorical
moments was to suggest that they were in a sense unremarkable, and that they

appear in the Euro-American feminist texts 'simply' because feminist visions emerged against the backdrop of this century in which fascism looms large. While the theoretical development of feminist theory, especially its relationship to versions of post-structuralist thought, have been subject to intense debate, the ways that the political events of the twentieth century altered the imaginative landscape of feminist politics have somewhat escaped attention. It is something of this history and its impact that are evoked by these rhetorical figures (the interloper, the collaborator with evil), and I believe they indicate the sense in which, within the many complexities of the twentieth century, its specificity as an age of fascisms has left its mark on any attempt to formulate political visions. Indeed, as Kristeva has remarked, it is for *this* specificity, *as well as* for its being a 'century of women', that the twentieth century will be known.

This is not to say that there were not other events, political movements, regimes and atrocities that were important to feminist movements and to women's lives around the globe in the last century. But there is something about how fascism is evoked within Euro-American feminist texts that gives pause. First, this history is remembered where there is the fear articulated that worthy political frameworks can be usurped. The temporary supplanting of democracy at its 'originary point', in Europe, is recalled in the characterization of arguments as so weakly formulated that if attacked they would offer no defence, as well as when people are criticized for being too certain of themselves, too unforgiving of their dissenters, too intolerant. Secondly, it is the knowledge of fascism's mobilizations of race-thinking, more than, say, the politics of expansionism or the aesthetic dimensions of fascism, that runs through these invocations of fascism within feminist theory and that, within what might otherwise have appeared to be a rather minor playground politics of name-calling, animates the issue of racism that has become central to feminist theoretical concerns. Of course race-thinking has a longer history and a wider reach than the twentieth-century fascisms to which it was integral, but it is so deeply combined with the figure of the fascist that in Nussbaum's invocation of 'collaborators with evil' who deny human dignity, for example, she summons up an image that draws part of its rhetorical force by an association with both totalitarianism and racism.

One way of responding to this (only somewhat self-imposed) injunction to think harder about feminist theory's relationship to fascism and race-thinking is to think genealogically. Taking some minor liberties with the notion of genealogy, starting from an affirmation of feminism, *Feminist Imagination* was intended to be an investigation into certain tributaries in the story that might be told of the course of twentieth-century feminist theory. That book adopted an approach somewhat closer to Nietzsche's genealogical impulse than Foucault's, simply because it is less systematic than Foucault's rather more restrained and scholarly approach would allow. The Nietzschean mode is more wayward, and more obviously purposeful; genealogies are not carried out completely innocently, and the routes one can follow are many. *Feminist Imagination* follows traces that illustrate my point that contemporary feminist thought is intimately attached to the history of thinking about racism and anti-Semitism in the twentieth century, not least because that history informs the fears, attachments and the horizons within which contemporary feminist debates imagine themselves. The argument is that following key debates and concepts within contemporary feminist theory leads one to issues, debates and concepts in the history of racism and anti-Semitism. Again, while this is unsurprising in so far as it could simply indicate how the appeal to humanistic or democratic values that linked abolitionism and feminism in the nineteenth century has been reconfigured in the link between issues of racism and sexism in the twentieth, this is not the argument. Instead, the argument is that feminist theoretical writing suggests that there is a political frame of reference beyond any strict focus on 'womanhood', one that makes issues of racism and the politics of fascism contextually important for understanding the way that much feminist argument has been and continues to be presented. The debate around essentialism and 'the body', for example, entered into feminist debate with an explicit connection to the politics of racism, as was clear in the feminist work of Diana Fuss or Elizabeth Spelman. The question of how to think the process of embodiment in non-essentialist ways, with due attention to its historical conditions of formation, entwines feminist thought with anti-colonial project of Frantz Fanon as well as, I would argue, Levinas's attempts to understand the appeal of National Socialism. Further, it is in the way that arguments are put together, the rich concepts that feminist theorists employ which, once recognized as such, cannot help but evoke, with their usage, the historical conditions that prompted those who form contemporary feminist theory's intellectual heritage to write about such things. There I discussed Hannah Arendt herself as an example of that heritage. For Arendt has been employed by Bonnie Honig, inter alia, within the development of the latter's feminist theories. Arendt's attention to the analysis of National Socialism, her entanglements with Heidegger, and her commentary on the racial politics of events in Little Rock in 1957 certainly trail her conception of agonistic politics and her key concept of appearance: does this disappear when she is used within feminist deployments? Or, to take another example I pursued in *Feminist Imagination*, isn't it relevant that Judith Butler uses the concept of mimesis in her development of a philosophy of gender, the concept central to Adorno and Horkheimer's discussion of anti-Semitism in *Dialectic of Enlightenment* (1986/1944) and also employed, even more importantly for Butler's heritage, by Sartre in *Anti-Semite and the Jew*?

Feminist Imagination, therefore, traced how issues of fascism as well as 'race' and racism reside within the feminist political imagination. These are really quite obvious connections, but while these connections have not been hidden, they had not been rehearsed or gathered together in order to make the kind of argument I was making there, where they could be viewed as a series of inter-related genealogies, as an 'uncovering' of a past easily traced but rarely presented. Somehow these connections seem to be left off frame within discussions of feminist thought, coming into focus again only when, as in Nussbaum's invention, they are evoked in heated exchange.

Fear and Rhetoric

Again, considering the work of Arendt might offer a way of approaching these evocations. As Dana Villa has argued in relation to the work of Hannah Arendt, and especially in relation to her image of the public realm as that which has to be preserved as the space of true freedom, *fear shapes arguments*. While her faith in the public realm might appear 'hopelessly romantic', Villa argues that it is important to recognize that her political thought was not built upon a nostalgic defence of democracy in the image of the Greek *polis*. Instead, she was reacting to the experience of terror under totalitarianism: 'Arendt's virtually life-long focus on the public sphere and the life of action grew out of her encounter with this radical negation of public reality and human freedom' (1999: 201). Reading Arendt, then, it helps to keep in mind that of which she was fearful, and what she was attempting to preserve and develop has to be considered against the backdrop of her analysis of totalitarianism.

In an attempt to redirect the energy indicated by the vitriol of a feminist debate premised on an accusation of 'dangerous thought', one might adopt Villa's stance and consider the fears that animate the arguments presented. In this case, as in others like it, one can say that the fears are apocalyptic in the sense that they fear 'the future end' (of feminist achievements and of democracy). But they cannot be dismissed because of their apocalyptic tone, since they are fears that have a historical basis, and in that sense have a rationality based on lessons of the past. Moreover, one could argue that these fears are *excessive* not in the sense that they exaggerate dangers ahead, but in the sense that although they are ostensibly focused on the internal concerns of theoretical argument, they simultaneously relate to and evoke external figures and markers. In arguments of this sort, then, someone or something external is suggested – the imagined interloper, for example, who is always off frame, waiting in the wings – and often historical examples are evoked if only dimly, used as veiled warnings. It is their excessive quality that makes it misguided to attempt to judge their validity from within the logic of the intervention itself. In making comment on them, one is not really debating the coherence of the arguments presented on the page, but engaging with the wider and murkier territory of rhetorical exchange, that is, the political, cultural and historical contexts that are evoked by the remarks.

As such the argument here is, like Villa's, that how we fear affects how we argue. These 'excessive' and 'external' contexts impact upon the rhetoric and therefore the logic of the arguments that are presented as if they were simply concerned with the rights and wrongs of how to develop the best kind of feminist theory. While it may be a subtle shift, it is instructive to ask of these debates not simply 'what is this feminist writer seeking to achieve and how?' but also 'what is this feminist writer seeking to avoid?' Which interloper, which threat, which horror – or indeed, which continuity – is our feminism to guard us against? Butler's principle focus suggests we need to guard against the repetitions of the present heterosexual matrix and its attendant patterning of social and asymmetrical relations that sets us into its patterns of identification. While Nussbaum does not disagree entirely with this fear, her argument alludes to another, for her, greater fear, because according to her there is an evil which will take advantage of a feminism too reserved in its judgements, too clever for the straight-talking reality of the world. This threat is one so elusive that we need also to challenge those who may seem to speak in the name of feminism, when in fact they unravel its defences; a threatening image that she shares to a certain degree with her anonymous critic who names this fear explicitly, if by analogy, as fascism.

Hopefully this characterization does not sound too glib, since the suggestion is that we look into these fears not in order to reject them as 'external' or 'unfounded', but quite the contrary to see how, as signs of certain animating features within debates in feminist theory, they need to be taken seriously. Thus Nussbaum places Butler's arguments according to the contexts of her understanding, where one can (indeed must) link an argument about the formation of gendered subjectivity to the defence of democracy and democratic values against its enemies. In order to make her critique of Butler, she performs rhetorical manoeuvres that attempt to persuade her readers that Butler's work is not just wrong and esoteric, but actually dangerous. She does so by placing Butler within a certain historical and cultural context and by summoning up the threatening image of the anti-democratic usurper as she simultaneously casts Butler herself as the collaborator.

As suggested above, to call feminist theoretical debates rhetorical does not mean they are untrue but it implies that there are always issues of persuasion at work. Feminist debate entails, as does any debate, attempts to persuade and convince an audience.[2] In a critique of deliberative democracy, Iris Marion Young argues that rhetoric is unavoidable in the public realm. Indeed, she argues that in her preferred model of democracy – communicative democracy – one must perforce include an understanding that rhetoric (which she discusses alongside along with story-telling and 'greeting'). She makes the point that, where Habermas attempts to distinguish between illocutionary and perlocutionary speech acts, and deliberative democratic theorists attempt to remove the passion of rhetoric through a focus on rational speech, one should not forget that democratic speech requires listeners as well as speakers. But, Young suggests, rhetorical speech is not distinguishable from rational speech. In Plato's *Gorgias*, Socrates suggests that rhetoricians aim to please rather than to convince through hard truths, but Plato shows

> in Socrates' person that there is an important erotic dimension in communication that aims to reach understanding, that persuasion is partly seduction. One function of rhetoric is to get and keep attention. The most elegant and truthful arguments may fail to evoke assent if they are boring. Humour, word-play, images and figures of speech embody and colour the arguments, making the discussion pull on thought through desire. (Young, 1996: 130–1)

As such, rhetoric appeals to the situatedness of the communication and constructs the speaker's relation to the audience. It would be a mistake to believe that the rhetoric of an intervention that accuses another of collaboration with an unnamed, but clearly undemocratic and non-egalitarian, evil is an intervention that makes assumptions about its audience any less than one who does not so name her fears. The emphasis is put this way around because Nussbaum accuses Butler of making assumptions about her audience – as liberal egalitarian sorts. Nussbaum assumes that people share her fears and her understanding that evil can be 'collaborated with' by an unsuspecting feminist philosopher, and she assumes further that she herself will not appear as the very threat she wishes to protect 'us' from. And she does so wrongly, as the anonymous author's essay demonstrates. The point is not that feminists are deploying mendacious tactics, but that they are seeking to be heard and to be persuasive. Figures of fear are routinely deployed in the course of making such arguments. Now although my own position is that Nussbaum may be deploying a version of innocence with respect to her own positioning, I have no reason to doubt the sincerity of her fears. Furthermore, while I have wanted to argue that the terms and imagery she evokes indicate the rhetorical nature of her critique, she can neither be castigated for being rhetorical, for reaching for images that express her historically based fears in order to make her case forceful, nor can she even be said to be *wrong* about the link between a theory such as Butler's and a danger of 'evil', since there are no criteria by which one might sensibly test that link. But while Nussbaum is not insincere, merely rhetorical, nor wrong, whosoever believes that her fears can only be made relevant on her 'side' of the debate is mistaken.

Feminist rhetoric in Nussbaum's mode attempts to suggest that it is possible to convince anti-egalitarian sorts of the errors of their ways by appeals to shared norms of equality, fairness, decency, dignity. But isn't it also the case that those in situations of conflict similarly appeal to those norms, but conclude their dispute differently? So it may be that Nussbaum is correct that

Butler's arguments could feasibly be used by someone on the extreme right of the political spectrum to legitimize their actions. On the other hand, they may just as conceivably legitimize their actions through appeals to norms. Thus, for example, members of the Orange Order in Northern Ireland might yet reveal a copy of *Gender Trouble* from under their jackets and sashes as they make their claim to perform their cultural identities by parading along certain nationalist routes for fear of their identities being lost. Often their language does come close to these anti-foundationalist positions. But equally, their claims based on the principles of dignity and respect that should be accorded their traditions employ language that is closer to a normative stance such as Nussbaum implies.

Thus in approaching debates about 'dangerous thinking', one needs to consider the contexts within which the interventions place themselves and their opponents as rhetorical strategies, not in order to dismiss the terms of the debate but to enable one to address the issue of dangerousness as a contingently formulated trope. In considering Nussbaum's reaction to Butler's work, one wonders about the relative lack of discussion in feminist theory around how imagined enemies are rhetorically drawn and incorporated into the repeated and heated debates around subject formation, resistance, agency, ethics and so on. For example, who is to say that the one against whom 'we feminists' need to prepare our argument is one who responds to normative statements better than arguments based on the radical contingency of the constitution of truths and identities? Is this always the language that will persuade our imagined political enemies? Are we at risk of being archaic, even nostalgic, for such an opponent against whom our only task is to clarify the force of a feminist social constructionism? Moreover, it is remarkable how quick theorists are to characterize anti-foundationalist positions as necessarily less rhetorically effective and more dangerous, when it is questionable, as Berube points out, whether the power of arguments that do not cite norms or foundations and that speak instead in terms of relations and contingencies have really been put to the test in political debate. Like those who worry that strategic essentialism involves a pretence rather than a conviction, Berube does not want to conclude that as an anti-foundationalist thinker he must use foundationalist claims wherever he intends to achieve his aims. He writes:

> I have no honest recourse but to believe that rhetorical strategies of persuasion, and nothing else, are the bases for human moral codes, then it is incumbent upon me to devise rhetorical strategies of persuasion that will convince people of the usefulness of this proposition. That means that the future of contingency is itself contingent: contingent, in this case, on forms of human agreement that anti-foundationalist progressives urgently need to discover – or invent. (2000: 153)

Perhaps it is this lack of debate about how theories relate to anticipated feminist fears, as much as how to depict feminist norms or aspirations, that creates disagreement amongst theorists.

To be rhetorical, since a space for such a performance has now been cleared: Couldn't we equally ask whether a contingent and non-foundational approach to normativity is any more risky than having cherished norms and foundations, manifestos perhaps and stable truths? And couldn't one place the fear of the end of feminist aspirations, of totalitarianism and of racism, say, into the mouths of those who critique normative approaches to social justice? What has been suggested here is that one has to answer affirmatively to both these questions. And if that argument has been (rhetorically) forceful enough, one might suggest further that the dangers inherent in living in a contingent world will not be avoided by seeking a positivity of good that does not entail an awareness of the fragility of constructing norms as rallying points. One is reminded of Jean-Luc Nancy's statement that

> If there is a hope of thinking, without which we would not even think, it does not consist in the hope of a total liberation of freedom that was to occur as the total mastery of freedom ... Today the threat of a devastation of existence alone has any positivity. (1993: 147)

Good, would that it did, does not share that positivity, and this is perhaps what fuels the fears that haunt these debates as well as what makes them, lamentably, rational. As Berube replies to his questioner, the threat of fascism will only be removed when there are no longer people who believe it a credible project. As long as there are such people, one is rational to fear and right to attempt to analyse ethnic absolutisms and race-thinking in its various contemporary and historical forms. But there is little comfort or gain to be had through a pretence that evil will attach itself to a particular theoretical style as if to a magnet, and little credibility to be given to one who claims the ability to see, to foresee and to comprehend the constitution of all the battles that face feminists and women, let alone democratic norms. Given the complexity and contingency of the world, it is unconvincing to suggest that any feminist theorist, of any ilk (neither the public architect of activism nor the philosophical guide) would be able to emerge with a fully convincing analysis of how best to articulate, achieve and protect feminist aspirations across all situations and for all times.

Judgement and Hope

The discussion brings us full circle in so far as it returns us to Arendt's question: thinking and its relationship or not with the avoidance of evil. For to be the recipient of rhetorical strategies is to be in the position of one who is or is not persuaded. And to consider rhetorical figures and the strategies of persuasion built with them, is to raise the question of their efficacy and the listeners' potential to be, or to refuse to be, convinced. It is to raise, in short, the question of how the recipient is placed to judge these attempts to persuade her.

In 'Thinking and Moral Considerations', Arendt makes the argument that although thinking deals with absences, has itself no appearance, and is in that sense neither political nor any guarantee, thinking does entail an internal dialogue which is related to conscience. When Socrates speaks of the need to be in 'harmony with oneself' as more important than the need to have multitudes agree with me, he relies upon a 'two-in-oneness' without which the notion of harmony does not make sense. In Socrates' teaching, Arendt finds the argument that, although my physical form may appear as one to others, to myself I am not one. The activity of thinking, and especially on matters of conscience, belies this. Arendt's point is that conscience responds to the other within, but only if one takes the time out of the business of life to *think*. For her, evil is not the result of not thinking, but thinking might have some potential to guard against it. In itself the activity of thinking creates no good, does not create anything, since its principle activity is to dissolve, to question (1984: 35). However, in extreme times, when there are those who are without conviction and those who 'are full of passionate intensity' (1984: 36), and when there is the danger that 'everybody is swept away *unthinkingly* by what everybody else does and believes in' (1984: 36), then the political implications of thinking come to the fore. Thinking has the ability to dissolve, and 'this destruction has a liberating effect on another human faculty, the faculty of judgement, which one may call, with some justification, the most political of man's mental abilities' (1984: 36). In this sense judgement 'realizes' thinking, making it appear (1984: 37), carrying it into the political world.

The optimism of Arendt's argument here, like Nancy's 'hope of thinking', rests on the image of a creativity without positivity, an internal dialogue that is necessarily informed by the political world outside, but that creates an internal movement that has its own potential in relation to both that subjectivity and that world. In relation to the argument developed here, the fact that there are rhetorical strategies that deploy their techniques of persuasion by drawing upon figures within a historically constituted and to a certain extent shared political landscape, does not prejudge anything about their reception. Of course, crucially, how one responds to and judges the persuasiveness of an argument is dependent upon the resources one has to think about it. First, too automatic a series of arguments and thought patterns, the less potential for thought and the less 'liberated', in Arendt's sense, is the judgement. Secondly, there is the limitation which Arendt herself implies elsewhere when she argues that judgement is always highly limited in so far as it takes place in relation to an anticipated community amongst whom 'I know I must finally come to some agreement.' (1963: 220) That is, Arendt argues that because judgement which 'rests on a potential agreement with others', 'the thinking process which is active in judging something is not, like the thought process of pure reasoning, a dialogue between me and myself, but finds itself always and primarily, even if I am quite alone in making up my mind, in an anticipated communication with others' (1963: 220). It is a specifically political ability, the ability to 'see things ... in the perspective of all those who happen to be present' (1963: 220). But as such it is also a problematic limitation, since, as the arguments of Wendy Brown (1995) and others such as Denise Riley (2000) have implied, the imagined communities of political speech are often deeply problematic.

To understand the political realm as one in which rhetorical strategies and figures circulate is therefore to remove the innocence of any form of public speech. Political argument, including that which takes place within theory, and even that which ostensibly aims to prompt thinking itself, cannot be exempted from such a critical analysis. Indeed, the only purpose of writing works such as this in which I am currently engaged is to provide resources that might make their way into that innermost conversation, which is anything but. Yet such public speech is not thinking itself, and while it floods thinking with its resonant images and suggested logics, so much so that the 'fact of thinking' is never again going to be grounds for certainty, and cannot sustain the anti-fascist hope it did for Arendt, the efficacy of public speech cannot be predicted either in its own terms or from the level of theory. That this is so is the tiniest chink of light under the door.

CHAPTER 5

Nausea's Potential? Genealogy and Politics

In place of the lines of determination laid down by laws of history, genealogy appears as a field of openings – faults, fractures, and fissures ... genealogy only opens possibilities through which various futures might be pursued.

Wendy Brown, *Politics Out of History*

How are we to reconcile the genealogically preoccupied subject with the Arendtian injunction – one that continues to resound – to be courageous, to stand out in the political realm, to rouse emotion and to make *demands*? If political endeavours are to be continually rerouted into explorations of their constitution, how, it might well be – and has been – objected, will we achieve anything? How can one seek a better world if all political demands, including one's own choices and passions, are placed under the scrutiny of the genealogist? Is not the genealogical figure an inwardly turned creature, too riven with self-accusations to be much use in the political realm, where actors unconcerned with genealogy need to be openly challenged with robust arguments and steadfast modes of argumentation?

In this chapter, I will argue that the accusation that genealogy reduces politics to critique has to be tackled head-on, and indeed, has to be accepted. However, acceptance of the argument that what Wendy Brown terms 'genealogical politics' is premised on an 'intellectual' interrogation of the realm of the political is not to accept its weakness. Indeed, it will be argued here that the worries expressed in these opening questions only make sense when politics is understood as a realm existing outside genealogy. Although genealogy is *intellectual* work, certainly, it is not to be understood as an endeavour that takes place outside – in the academy, say – or 'after' politics, for to proceed in that vein is to tarry with a very narrow notion of politics. But what, then, is genealogy's political potential?

Genealogical politics presents itself as a political intervention precisely because it is interrogative. Its comprehension of the constitution of what counts as political refutes the notion that politics is the present meeting of contrasting opinions about how to proceed into the future (as in a Habermasian speech-situation). By contrast, genealogy works with an understanding of politics as about different modes of connecting and disconnecting (things, people and processes), and it is also therefore about different modes of mobilizing or *enacting* this present. Genealogy attends to that which, often silently, animates and sustains the present(ed) understandings. In this way, a genealogical analysis traces the constitution of this realm, how it has developed and is sustained. But it is not about uncovering secrets. It is rather about interrogating the connections made within political argument, unfolding what has been folded there, tracing the lines of logic, light, subjectification that have come to coalesce in the political realm or event. In this way, as Brown and others have argued, the genealogist presents an analysis of the constitution of the political that is itself political. And while it must always be understood as provisional rather than true, the acceptance of its own provisionality is not a weakness but a strength in so far as its challenge is always to show the similarly partial and specific constitution of the claims and interventions it interrogates.

As a response to the initial worries expressed by our imagined interlocutor, this argument has coherence: indeed it has become a sort of standard response. However, I will suggest that there is a problematic expressed in these questions that is not entirely satisfied by such a response. This concerns a deeper division arranged less between the traditional, presentist and state-centred image of politics and the genealogists' interrogative approach to the realm of the political, and more between different philosophical approaches to understanding how genealogy might, or could possibly, relate to the notion of pursuing different future possibilities. As articulated by Wendy Brown in the quotation at the head of this chapter, genealogy's self-proclamation as political is related to the sense in which, through its revelation of the present's radical contingency, it opens up possibilities otherwise unknown, unavailable or untapped. Its principle method is figured, ultimately, as a process of inducing a sickness or swooning: inducing a *nausea* that results from the revelation that the ways of the world are not set and might well go on differently. In this chapter I want to pursue this potential of nausea and to ask whether there is more that needs to be clarified here in relation to the question of the political potential of genealogical practice.

I will suggest that when genealogical approaches construe the realm of the political as an endlessly enfolded domain, and the task of its interrogation the unravelling of the coextensivities that have produced and sustain present configurations, the nature of the possibilities that might arise there can be differently understood. In debating how they are to be conceived, the genealogist's ability to demonstrate them is certainly under scrutiny; but that ability, I suggest, is not only about the talent and skill of the genealogist but about how one understands the very possibility of such demonstration, and therefore the possibility of opening up Brown's 'other possibilities'. I will explore this by pursuing a seeming similarity between genealogy and the work of Michel Callon and Bruno Latour, in order to suggest that there is a certain tension that arises here that might give in turn a different take on what makes genealogy political. This line of questioning will push at the deepest assumptions of genealogical work. But here we are getting too far ahead of ourselves. First, let us return to what I called the 'standard response' to those attacking genealogy in relation to 'the political', what amounts to a principled shoring up of its perspective.

Genealogical Politics as Vertiginous Knowledge: Nausea's Potential

Wendy Brown has suggested that although genealogy does not lead to conventional political demands, genealogy is political because it leads to a new knowledge, a 'vertiginous knowledge when developed within the culture it aims to unravel' (2001: 98). This knowledge is that for which Nietzsche called when he called for a genealogy of morality, one born of an investigation that begins from a belief that is a non-belief, or a belief in nothing. That is, genealogy begins from an assumption that there is nothing 'behind' things – no gods, no essences, no absolutes. Everything can and should be questioned in order to begin to see how what *is* has been 'made up' against the emptiness of all possibilities. There is, as William Connolly has described, a certain sensibility implicit in adopting a genealogical approach. Connolly quotes Foucault's argument that 'we have to [dig deeply to] show how things have been historically contingent, for such and such a reason intelligible but not necessary. We must make the intelligible appear against a background of emptiness and deny its necessity. We must think that what exists is far from filling all possible spaces' (Connolly, 1998: 114). The method of genealogy is about adopting a certain attitude to the past, a pathos of distance; it is also about learning to *ask questions* of present truths. To give present truths histories, genealogies, is to seek an understanding of the 'conditions and circumstances in which they grew' (1967/1887: 20). From this endeavour, these other 'possible spaces' emerge.

Just as Nietzsche presented himself as one who had 'ceased to look for the origin of evil *behind* the world' in order to ask 'under what conditions did man decide these value judgements good and evil? *And what value do they themselves possess?*' (Preface, 1967/1887: 17), so Foucault argued that to listen to history would be to reject metaphysical answers in favour of the fabrication of things: 'if the genealogist refuses to extend his faith in metaphysics, if he listens to history, he finds there is "something altogether different" behind things: not a timeless and essential secret but the secret that they have no essence, or that their essence was fabricated in a piecemeal fashion from alien forms' (1997/1984: 371). Genealogy rejects teleologies in favour of the piecemeal, which, like the rejection of the metaphysical in favour of physical materialities, leads in both Nietzsche's and Foucault's cases, to an attention on the human, the 'all too human' forces. We have given the notions of good and bad, good and evil to ourselves, Nietzsche swipes (in *Ecco Homo* where he summarizes the *Genealogy of Morals*), taking Christianity to task for its manufactured ideals, 'manufactured in a workshop that stinks of so many lies' (1967/1908: 47) as his imagined interlocutor puts it. What Nietzsche's genealogy presents is an alternative history, one that asserts that the notions of 'good' and 'bad' operate as a rationalization undergirding what is actually the human delight in witnessing the punishment of one's opponents. Indeed, the very notion of justice might be regarded as based in a spirit of *ressentiment*.

So Nietzsche certainly intends to induce a vertigo in his genealogy of morality: on the one hand, he argues, notions of good and bad were developed by the 'nobles' – the noble affirms himself and the negative concept comes afterwards, as that which is lowly and common. The concepts of good and bad are the self-inventions of the nobles. On the other hand, the man of *ressentiment* will also develop a notion of the good, but his 'good' emerges after his concept of evil developed: 'picture the "enemy" as the man of *ressentiment* conceives him – and here precisely is his deed, his creation: he has conceived "the evil enemy" "the Evil One" and this in fact is his basic concept, from which he then evolves, as an afterthought and pendant, a "good one" – himself!' (1967/1887: 39). Thus there is a battle set up between versions of morality: good is perspectival, not because it infinitely varies, but in so far as it varies in relation to the specific arrangements of its development.

In enquiring of the politics of the one who speaks the vertiginous knowledge delivered genealogically, in wondering about the task of politics co-emergent with that knowledge, it is important to note that in genealogical critique there is no room for the adoption of the position of underling. Those articulating their politics from such a position are eyed with suspicion from within a Nietzschean stance. The man of *ressentiment* is 'poisoned' by his *ressentiment*. He is far from appealing, a weak figure who attempts to turn his weakness into something meritorious (1967/1887). This is an argument that has been noted and debated within feminist theory, in so far as there has been a legitimate worry that feminist activism and feminist theory might be cast as *ressentiment* (see Bell, 1999; Stringer, 2003), and that that *ressentiment* might be promoted by a capitalist logic with which feminism becomes unwittingly complicit (Hennessey, 2000).

Rebecca Stringer (2003) makes a wonderfully nuanced analysis of how feminists might engage with the notion of *ressentiment* and argues ultimately that there are generative possibilities of the figure of *ressentiment*, provided that it is understood that its railing against democracy's failures contains *both* the contradictory consequences of the impulse to blame. Nietzsche laments the comprehension of the world wrought through a language of 'blame'; but within an emancipatory imaginary, argues Stringer, it has the potential to envision a positively different world (2003: 371). Stringer challenges us not to use Nietzsche's 'diagnosis' of the man of *ressentiment* in priestly fashion, that is, in ways that rush to condemn feminism for its regressive and mimetic postures. Rather, one might recognize the dangers of *ressentiment* while acknowledging that the notion of 'victim' can also operate more creatively and courageously, as a vehicle through which 'socio-political being may be opened to contingency … [such that] the category 'victim' may be regarded not as inimical to agency but as a source of agency' (2003: 376–7). Keith Ansell Pearson also points out that there is an ambiguity (or a paradox) surrounding Nietzsche's man of *ressentiment* because his 'poisoning' also makes for his development. Nietzsche suggests a cleverness will develop in the man of *ressentiment*, while intelligence becomes less and less essential in the noble's luxurious but languid life (1967/1887: 38–9). For Nietzsche it is the slave revolt in morality that will introduce intelligence – *Geist* – into history, then, where 'intelligence' signals cunning, mimicry, self-control, patience (Ansell Pearson, 1997: 18).

It is here that one sees how the genealogical subject yields a vision of political subjectivity modelled in Nietzsche on the potentialities of slave morality. As opposed to the bravery, the courage of the public actor emphasized in Arendt or the reflexive communicative actor of Habermas, the principle quality of this political actor is intelligence and patience. And in Nietzsche this figure is *explicitly* contrasted with the one who makes bold political demands for the equality of themselves with those whom they oppose. Let us be clear: not *all* bold statements are equivalent and rendered suspect. But claims to a share, claims of being left out that are made by the one so evaluated, are ripe for genealogical scrutiny.[1]

In Foucault – Brown and Connolly, too, in so far as they are indebted to Nietzsche – the political subjectivity that genealogy yields is an intelligent, patient and insistent figure. Genealogy is *intellectual* work. It is presented as methodical, rigorous and painstaking, but ever attuned to the possibility of its own inaccuracies, omissions or misrepresentations. It may be bold and even shocking in its offering of new perspectives, but it also invites intelligent critique, keenly aware of its own provisionality. Because it is intellectual work, 'genealogical politics' has to struggle against the criticism that it entails a reduction of politics to questions, and intervention to critique, making its nomenclature contradictory in its own terms. Mindful of the potential for such a dismissal, Brown insists that in its denaturalizing of objects and situations and in its treatment of time – that is, more 'gravely' (2001: 103) in so far as it attends to time's power as a field of forces in space – the genealogist 'reorients the relationship of history to political possibility' (2001: 103). Brown argues that genealogy shows how:

although the present field of political possibility is constrained by its histories, those histories are themselves tales of improbable, uneven, and unsystematic emergence, and thus contain openings for disturbance. In place of the lines of determination laid down by laws of history, genealogy appears as a field of openings – faults, fractures, and fissures ... genealogy only opens possibilities through which various futures might be pursued. (2001: 104)

At this point, it is tempting to suggest that since this is the key to the politics of genealogy, it is possible to render an equivalence of sorts between this intellectual demonstration and the forms of public demonstration more routinely understood as 'political'. Through their demonstration, both interrupt in order to point to other possibilities. As Andrew Barry nicely argues, demonstration has a number of meanings that are worth bearing in mind when thinking 'politics' and 'resistance'. As well as the idea that a demonstrator is one who protests, acting as a riposte or '[marker] of the unacceptability of another's actions' (2001: 177), the term 'demonstrator' also has an earlier historical sense. In the Middle Ages the demonstrator had a particular function in the anatomy lecture theatre, namely to point out the feature of the body about which the lecturer was speaking, and thereby to help clarify and disseminate anatomical knowledge. As Barry argues, to be this kind of demonstrator was to aid in the transfer and dissemination of knowledge to a wider audience via a *technical* practice. This sense of the term continues in contemporary science education wherever students are assisted in the laboratory by a 'demonstrator', one who points out to them what they are witnessing, and what they are expected to discover and understand (Barry, 2001: 177). And if such an equivalence is not enough to silence those who scoff at genealogy's purported intervention, might not one still these critics by risking the suggestion that genealogical knowledge prompts a critique that may lead to criticism that may lead to political demands for change, in a fairly conventional image of the politicization of knowledge.

However, advocates of genealogy hesitate around such a rendering of genealogical practice. As opposed to this image of how knowledge becomes programmatic, how it informs policy or wider political calls for change, there is no escaping the idea that genealogy's first impulse is to prompt thought and to continually prompt thought rather than the demands and protests that are conventionally accepted as political action. For while there is much, especially in Foucault's approach, that suggests what is *not* likely to be politically efficacious and what is *not* necessary in prompting sociopolitical change – there is no need to seek for total comprehension to effect change, nor for total revolution to achieve it (Brown, 2001: 113) – these negatives are not followed by arguments as to what genealogies demand should be done. If there is a polemicization – a translation of genealogical argument into the polemics more readily recognized as 'political' speech and intervention – it is not the genealogical work that can claim a causal role. Nor can it be held accountable for that utilization, still less its consequences. It *cannot* be held accountable; and nor, likewise, can it claim any successes in that realm. The genealogist can seek neither gratitude nor rewards for a role in prompting change. Correlatively, the political actor can never be beholden to a genealogical account of the phenomena to which her action is directed, and cannot be called to account by the genealogist for the accuracy of his or her translation of genealogical knowledge into 'political action'. Genealogies *may* enter truth claims within the socio-political field – hence Foucault's much quoted claim that while his work should be approached as fictions, fictions can nevertheless be plausibly '*made* to work within truth' (Morris and Patton, 1979: 75; Gordon, 1980: 193) – but to think of them as the rationale, projects or anchors of political action would be somewhat perverse in their own terms: they do not demonstrate in this sense.

It is because genealogies produce not the steadfast determined actor of the political or revolutionary arena, but the vertiginous subject unsettled and made queasy by a knowledge that undermines present truths and present arrangements, that genealogy remains incompatible with polemicization or the politicization of its conclusions. It necessarily underdetermines any response to its vertiginous effects. Indeed, it resists the notion that its work translates into political demands for, as suggested above, the political actor given to polemics makes the genealogist winch. The shorthands of political rhetoric and posturing condense the long (and broad) stories upon which genealogy insists. Moreover, the pitfalls of political argument are many, and polemics themselves necessarily prompt genealogical interrogations (see Brown on conviction, 2001: 91–5). Thus the courageous political actor that Arendt describes is less a model for the theorist's admiration, still less her emulation, and more a figure requiring her considered analysis. Genealogy takes instead the position of the witness and analyst. As Brown concludes, the proper place for the political theorist is not within but as the 'interlocutor' of the political domain (2001: 120). Happier in the posing of questions, genealogy must live with its underdeterminations and consequently has also to abide with the accusation that its politics – that is 'genealogical politics' – has all the potential to become indistinguishable from critique. It has to endure these ripostes precisely because they have a certain and necessary accuracy about them.

That said, an entirely legitimate question might follow: are there any rules to distinguish a genealogical interlocutor from the next intelligent critic? If the political theorist is properly the interlocutor of the political domain in Brown's sense, are there particular questions s/he should ask? If genealogy is about the unfolding of what has been enfolded in the present, about showing the contingency of the relations sustained there, are there clues as to how it might proceed in this task?

While it is proper that genealogy has no rules, no method as such, it is also hard to deny that there are certain modes of attending to 'political machines', as Andrew Barry (2001) has termed them, which seem to accompany the genealogical sensibility. In seeking to comprehend and question the constitution of politics.

Foucault's work itself encouraged a very particular attention to the *how* of political government, to the specific rationalities, technologies and geometries at stake in the domain under consideration. Wendy Brown, rightly and usefully, emphasizes the importance of the term 'political rationality' in Foucault's work, noting his debt to Weber in his echo of the argument that studies of political rationalities are a principle way to understand how the state functions to legitimize its actions 'releasing' its need to use violence (2001: 114). In seeking to enquire as to which rationalities are being put to work within a particular social-political configuration, Foucault seeks to map the geometries of power relations at work, to ask as to the constraints that rationalities effect but also of the creations and creativities they produce and sustain, the ways of thinking and acting they subtend. For Foucault, modern political configurations were best approached as practices that simultaneously individualize – that is, produce individuals as specific elements – and organize individuals into groups. Even – and perhaps especially – where these individualizing processes may seem to preserve precious identities and freedoms, these same processes can be understood to constrain and orchestrate their expression, arranging their form and patterning (Rose, 2000). Figures of resistance are always to be viewed in the context of the political rationalities that reign, therefore, whether one wishes to argue that they concur or diverge from the possibilities constituted through those rationalities. This already suggests a number of things to which the genealogical interlocutor of the political is attentive, around which s/he produces her analytic interrogation. One might even begin to list a number of aspects of 'the political' to which a good genealogical account would attend: the historical development of the rationales and tropes employed in the jostle to politicize; the management of the process of interruption integral to politicization, with its attendant potential for violence; the utilization of technologies of communication that accompany the orchestration of the political domain (Barry, 2001); the fragile process by which a witness is summoned and even a 'community' constituted at the site of the political event; the new connections, concepts, calculations and figures that emerge through the processes of entangling or disentangling that inhere in political rhetoric and actions.

This list is not exhaustive. But the point here is not to develop the exhaustive list but to argue that at the crux of all of these tasks – and any further ones we might add – is an attention to rationales and processes of categorizing, arranging or cutting, in other words to the limits imposed and orders established, and thence to the possibilities that have been eclipsed, displaced, forgotten, neglected, rendered unliveable or unthinkable (these are not equivalent and the different implications will become important as we shall see below). In effect, what is suggested by advocates of genealogy is that if one attends to what has been pushed into the shadows, remaindered, rendered non-existent, the present is revealed as a collection of contingent dispositifs, labyrinthine webs of no absolute necessity. That dizzying revelation is political, the argument runs, because it makes available a glimpse of the *real* possibilities that present reality performatively denies. That is, of what could have been and what might still be. In other words, what Wendy Brown implies when she argues that genealogy's nausea is politically productive is that it might stand one before all the hitherto unconsidered but nevertheless real 'possibilities through which various futures might be pursued' (2001: 104).

From Externalities to Anxiety, and from Anxiety to Actualization

One way to understand this process of unfolding might be to think of it as akin to the attention to 'externalities' found in the work of Michel Callon (see, e.g. Callon, 1998) who seeks to bring this concept from economic theory into conversation with social science. Callon explains that externalities – either 'negative', as in the emission of poisonous gases from a factory, or positive, as in the patenting of new designs that others may then use – are effects one activity or relationship has for other actors uninvolved in that activity or relationship. In economic theory, the organization of resources and efficiency means that the implications of externalities are of utmost interest. It becomes important to know whether calculations about a factory's costs are ignoring social costs of its pollution of its surrounding area, just as it becomes important to know whether the fact that patents benefit competitors might be discouraging investment in innovation. In a different language, micro-sociological approaches have had a similarly long-standing interest in how interactions – an economic exchange, a legal contract, a dinner party, a chance encounter – can be understood as *framed* (in Goffman's sense). And since, in accordance with Goffman's now classic argument, framing renders an 'isolated' intelligibility or quality to interactions which are *in fact* sustained by the various human and non-human actors that enable them to take place, each framing nevertheless indicates its dependency on the outside world. It indicates in other words, that 'the outside world is also present' (Callon, 1998: 250). The distinction between the two disciplines, to Callon's mind, is that economics has tended to regard framing as the norm, as both ubiquitous and desirable, and has focused on the 'overflows' from the frames as exceptions to be measured and channelled with appropriate investments. Social science has, typically, been interested in highlighting the omnipresence of the world and arguing its indissociability from the scene of interactions in which any given actor is involved. Callon's perspective develops from insights of both disciplines, focusing on the analysis on externalities and the 'overflows' of interactions. Given that every frame, even a legal contract, depends upon the existence of a plethora of elements of the world 'outside' – concepts, materials and institutional arrangements (in the case of contracts, for example, legal concepts, procedures and law courts) – these elements can be understood to both limit and to act as 'potential conduits for overflows' (Callon, 1998: 254). They close around an interaction while simultaneously opening it up onto the world. Indeed, argues Callon, from this perspective the attempt to plug overflows systematically, to suppress all connections and eradicate externalities would not be possible. Nor would it be desirable, because 'without overflows, it would not be possible to add value locally.' (1998: 255)

In economics, as the constructivist sociologist would predict, the identification of overflows necessary for coordinating exchange becomes controversial. The economic approach wishes to provide information and mechanisms by which externalities can be foreseen and measured; yet it is immediately faced with the difficulties of so doing (Callon, 1998: 256–7). First, the reality of the overflow has to be proven and mapped, then, the link from a (not necessarily pre-existing) group of those affected back to the source has to be proven and demonstrated; thereafter the impact has to be quantified by legitimate and recognized instruments, which may have to be created for the purpose. The constructivist sociologist's critical role, according to Callon, must surely be in highlighting the importance of these operations to identify and measure overflows, encouraging a questioning of the mechanisms used to create frames and the procedures required to render the overflows knowable.

For Callon it seems that the analysis has an aim beyond providing coherent analysis of 'what happens'; it is the promotion of renegotiations and improved, (because) recalculated, interactions. The level of difficulty involved in this work is considerable, he recognizes, especially in those situations he terms 'hot', those controversial instances where nothing – the existence, nature, measures or direction of the 'overflows' – is agreed upon. But while this hot world, this increasingly complicated and interconnected world, is becoming difficult to 'cool' enough to allow for the improved reframing and negotiation of interactions (1998: 263), Callon suggests that this complication does not render this difficult work is impossible. What it does mean is that more work will inevitably be drawn into the identification of externalities, without being able to proceed to the reframing and renegotiation stage. And this identification of externalities is of course highly charged, not least because that which one might wish to avoid in the drawing up of contracts[2] – the resort to forms of interaction based on resolution through strength or violence – needs itself to be subject to a historical analysis. That is, to imagine the negotiation of exchange as promoting civilization is to continue an Enlightenment tradition that spins a particular tale, one that underplays the contract as a site at which identities and understandings are not only negotiated but are formed and imposed; there is a complicity therefore with the sort of foundational violences that contracts may have.

So Callon paints a picture of analyses that attend carefully to the site of a negotiation as complicated and, in some instances at least, as an inherently political site. He argues that much contemporary work – by economists and sociologists, whether driven by needs of the market negotiations or by concerns of critical analysis – will inevitably become entangled in the complicated task of identifying the dual role – as block and as conduit – of the various frames to which they attend. And he suggests that there cannot be a bracketing out of this political aspect even if the aim is a renegotiated contract (as opposed to a sociological analysis) since there remains a need to be vigilantly critical, as sociologists have been, of how framing – its assumptions, techniques and its logics – takes place.

It is not difficult to see the resonance that this approach, drawn from a long sociological tradition and translated through Callon's juxtaposition with economic theoretical concerns, has with genealogical approaches. The emphasis on locating externalities and the directions and impacts of 'overflows' might be likened to the process of tracing the lines of the *dispositif* that arrange, constrain and impose form and meaning on their dependent elements. Beginning with the sustained elements, genealogy traces their constitution and configuration across time and space. Thus the genealogist is similarly interested in understanding any chosen site of interaction or concern as constituted, as 'arising' out of the web whose folds and contortions deliver it into existence. Like Callon's deployment of the notion of externalities, the radical manoeuvre is always to relocate the unit or singularity within the lines of its present arrangements, to illuminate its dependences, its extensions, its shadows, by considering what is placed outside the frame. And if 'what is placed outside the frame' has a vagueness to it, that is because it can indeed be anything at all (Latour 2004: 124) and will need to be discovered in the empirical work of tracing. In both Callon's work and in genealogy, then, the injunction to follow the unfurled relations in the specificities of the instance under consideration is a method or perhaps a politics, but not a theory about where this might lead. Indeed, as Latour says in his reflections on the actor-network theory (which he and Callon popularized in the 1980s and 1990s; see, e.g. 1981), ANT was a method that, like many of the anti-essentialist movements that characterized the end of the twentieth century, was premised on the notion that one could achieve more 'by following circulations ... than by defining entities, essences, or provinces' (Latour 1999: 20).

Implicit in this emphasis on circulation, fluidity and space, was always the displacement of modernist schemas, argues Latour, as ANT opposed itself to religion (theology), to any notion of an outside (nature) or an inside (psychology) and indeed any political schemas that fixed identities, groups and boundaries. Although paradigmatically expanding attention beyond that which is 'human, all too human' to include non-human actors in this earthly entanglement, ANT shares the Nietzschean impulse to bring things to earth, to foray long and hard but only into the worldly origins of things. Latour also shares the correlative distaste for a politics that is set in advance, such as that based on a 'perverse taste for the margins' as he puts it in *We Have Never Been Modern* (1993), where, for example, 'the local' is automatically preferred to 'the global' without proper attention to how these terms operate in a series of specific connections in each instance of their usage. To interrogate the *value* of value judgements remains crucial to the analysis.

Latour's more recent work explicitly maintains that this tracing of how things come into existence gives the task a *moral* thrust. Speaking of the role of 'moralists' in relation to scientific processes, Latour argues that the vigilance of the moralists is not the application of abstract rules, nor is it to block developments; rather it is to promote the appropriate witnesses for any particular 'candidate to existence'. A jury, Latour suggests, that attends to the specificities of the action under consideration so that whatever emerges there (a new mapping of a problem, a new hypothesis, a new thing of some sort) is scrutinized in that specificity: 'each candidate to existence is evaluated by a jury corresponding to its own recalcitrant problem, *not* through indifferent questions raised for other purposes' (Latour, 2004: 158). There is no blueprint for these evaluations, just as there is no theory of ANT. All that one can say *in general* about this task is that it injects a constant *anxiety*. The moralists feed 'a constant anxiety over rejected facts, the eliminated hypotheses, the neglected research projects – in short, everything that might make it possible to seize the opportunity to bring new entities into the collective that are at the limit of the sensibility of the instruments' (Latour, 2004: 158).

What is the relation of Latour's *anxiety* to Brown's vertiginous *nausea?*

Like genealogy's propensity to induce nausea, Latour's moralists provoke anxiety through an insistence that attention be focused on what has been pushed out of consideration. Anxiety results from a process akin to genealogy's unfolding because where Foucault would have understood objects to emerge through a process of folding so that genealogy seeks in turn to trace the lines of the *dispositif*, for Latour '"internalisation" is also always a work of "externalisation"' (Fraser, 2006: 63) so that the work of morality is to focus attention on the exterior that has constituted the object (Latour, 2004: 125). It is in order that the artifice of what is created is not only viewed 'from within' (Latour, 2004: 158) and at the expense of those things excluded that the work of moralists becomes consonant with politicians. Each time a political actor claims to be representative, the moralist asks about the 'they' that has been externalized, that explicit and collective decisions have placed outside the account, cast as insignificant, decided to do without (Latour 2004: 124). Viewing things excluded anew causes all one's assumptions to be re-evaluated, calling into question the procedures by which one has established one's truth (or elements or frame) as contingent and unnecessary. Latour implies further that this anxiety-provoking work of 'the moralists' might *interrupt* something, chiming with the way that I argued genealogy might also work as a non-productive, non-directive, ethics (in Chapter 3).

There are however some key problems in rushing the connection between these two bodies of work, for there are still matters of debate, ones which mean that we need to think again about how we understand the lines of the *dispositif*, and in particular about how we think about the process of actualization by which some 'candidates to existence' achieve presence and are sustained while others do not, or appear perhaps but limpingly, in haunted fashion.

When one is staring into Connolly's abysmal 'emptiness', one swoons (Brown) or is properly anxious (Latour). But it is also implied in Latour that this anxiety might be resolved, or that the abyss might be *mapped* so that in turn, it might have implications for a way of proceeding (be that a research programme, a political movement, a technique, whatever); it might (re)begin a productive *reconsideration* about the direction or constitution advocated. Certainly Callon implies that for the economist-reader of his piece, there is the promise that ideally a newly renegotiated interaction might result. Ultimately, Latour's politics is a politics of *reality* (Latour, 2004: 160; Fraser, 2006: 64) in so far as he shares implication that however complicated a task, it is possible to point to the exteriors, as Callon points to the externalities, that are necessary but 'framed out' of the phenomena under scrutiny. As Mariam Fraser notes, Latour can offer his reader examples as to what has been rendered 'exterior' and 'these kinds of example point to a curious emphasis on what is already able to be imagined' (2006: 64); the task becomes one of *demonstrating* that these exteriors are in fact crucial in the production of this frame, this phenomena or singularity.

But what lies beyond the lines of the '*dispositif*' is surely much less traceable than this not least because, as Deleuze points out, lines of light (that is, the *conditions* of visibility) are themselves part of the lines of the deployment. The dimensions of the abyss, of the 'emptiness', cannot be known. One might suggest that what has *not* been brought to presence exists, but it could only exist *virtually*. Latour sets his position against one in which fact and value are separated and moral values are thought to offer a 'salvation from on high' in relation to the mere 'matters of fact'; he suggests instead that in practice all the transcendence that is needed 'to escape from the straitjacket of immanence is found there, on the outside, *within reach*' (2004: 125, emphasis added). But can our ways of asking about what has not been granted existence be simply a pointing to those things excluded, these other considerations or objects, existing, seemingly unconnected but connected nonetheless, via a route that analysis will reveal takes us from here to there, to them, 'over there'?

As Latour himself has argued, there has been a muting of the influence of Deleuze and Guattari on ANT,[3] such that, for example, the network came to mean '*an instantaneous unmediated access* to every piece of information' (1999: 15, emphasis added). Like the political science version of Foucault's govern-mentality, which, admitting of no nuanced genealogy, tends to regard products and subjects as smoothly produced through the logics of political rationalities alone, this implied access to constitutive 'externalities' makes the task of the theorist an empirical-realist project.[4] With this turning away from any inkling of the concept of virtuality, no attention is given to a *virtual* reality that accompanies the actual phenomenon under discussion, so that it is easy to forget that the *dispositif* cannot be posited against a field of alternative possibilities (past or present) open to *demonstration*.

In other words, if one allows for the creativity of *processes of actualization* it means that while different possibilities are *real*, this *is not* the same, and *cannot* be the same, as saying they are demonstrable. This virtual is not, let us be clear, any less *historical* than actual events since actual events develop as solutions whereas virtual or ideal events are 'embedded in the conditions of the problem' (Deleuze, 2004/1994: 189). The process of actualization constitutes one solution to the historical problem it 'solves' (DeLanda, 2002: 156). But the virtual is necessarily outside the grip of the historian. Latour gets somewhat closer to this way of thinking when he writes about the externalized entities putting the collective 'in danger', or 'coming back to haunt' (2004: 124–5). Latour might be taken to imply that these external entities are maintained – *potentially* one might say – *within* the 'interior', as in where he speaks of the possibility that what has been externalized *appealing*, coming back to 'knock at the door of the collective' (2004: 125), or the interior having 'a reminder of the artifice by means of which it was designed' (2004: 160). But, as Mariam Fraser argues, Latour's indebtedness to Whitehead does not extend to the latter's argument that the process of becoming involves the exclusion of alternative *potentiality* (Whitehead 1978/1929: 67, quoted in Fraser, 2006: 65) such that 'in so far as the excluded things are important in your experience, *your modes of thought are not fitted to deal with them*' (Whitehead 1985/1926: 73, quoted in Fraser, 2006: 65). Latour does seem to retain some sense of quality control carried out by 'the moralists', such that the value of those things that attain existence is questioned by the moralists' deceleration, a deceleration they institute by asking about the process by which such-and-such attained existence.

Just as Fraser queries the task allocated to Latour's moralists, so too, if we allow for such a 'virtual' reality, would a change be suggested for the assumptions of genealogical work. It suggests that it is wrong to assume that *any* solution or effect might have developed. The possibilities for how something appears, in other words, is not against the backdrop of *all* possibilities, as the rhetoric of genealogy often implies, but only against the backdrop of the possibilities that *pertain to it*. Another way to make this point would be to argue that an entity, situation or mode-of-being – and all three simultaneously imply each other – carries the potential to become differently, and that potentiality 'belongs' to it whichever 'solution' actualizes itself. In Agamben's sense then, a thing 'maintains its own privation' (1999: 182), carrying the possibility of its *own* non-Being with it, its potential not-to-be (emphasis added, 1999: 182–4). How things become is not arbitrary in relation to what those things *are*, that is, but nor is it either essential or predictable.[5] What shadows them is not some other thing or a rejected, bracketed possibility in the shadows, but other *real but unactualized* possibilities that are like a shadow only in the sense that they are precisely joined to *this* thing. From this perspective other concepts are immediately placed under re-evaluation as well. The concept of foreclosure, for example, cannot be understood as an operation of power alone, since what can be foreclosed can only be that which is held in potentiality with, and is – in this sense only – *of* the thing.

If, with these arguments in mind, one returns to Brown's notion of 'future possibilities', it seems clear that the analysis of the present's *dispositifs* cannot endorse a 'politics of reality', in the sense discussed above, that would be able to point to the remaindered entity or problematic, since these are the things by definition not granted existence. But genealogy has also to guard against a position in which the impossibility of knowing or tracing the lines of the *dispositif* becomes resigned to *this* reality.

Genealogical work is political, but it might be better to understand it, therefore, not as directing or imagining the future nor even as giving glimpses of other possibilities but as itself partaking in the environment within which the phenomena at stake disappears, survives, transforms or mutates. Indeed, Wendy Brown approaches such a position when she suggests that genealogical work may *incite* other possibilities into emergence (2001: 104). The work itself might function performatively in this sense (see also Urry and Law, 2004). It might become part of the environment within which an 'other possibility' is created or not. But in becoming part of the ecology, even partaking in the processes of composition, it cannot be figured as doing so except in some relation to the potentiality of that which is under consideration, without being tethered in this way. And the process of planning this addition, even of calculating the proportions of its success or failure, even *retrospectively*, is fraught with difficulties.

Such a reappraisal of genealogy throws into some doubt the very concept of performativity, for to begin to use the language of potentiality and processes of actualization in this way is to change certain key philosophical assumptions that gave rise to the concept. In the next chapter I want to suggest that one way to consider this is through the different understandings of creativity at stake, and to unpick the points of convergence and of contrast, in order to investigate the specificities of the challenge to the concept of performativity contained in this line of thought.

CHAPTER 6

Performativity Challenged?
Creativity and the Return of Interiority

Being differs with itself immediately, internally. It does not look outside itself for an other or a force of mediation because its difference rises from its very core, from 'the explosive internal force that life carries within itself'.

Gilles Deleuze, 'Bergson's Conception of Difference'

Within feminist theory, as well as in other areas of thought, certain terms, hitherto rejected, bracketed or even forbidden are being reassessed and reanimated anew. 'Ontology', 'materiality', 'evolution' are being reasserted with an enthusiasm in seeming contradiction with radical perspectives of the recent past. Of course, with such complex terms at stake, these reassessments are not all of the same ilk; nevertheless, it is remarkable that one now finds some of the most eminent feminist theorists engaged in explorations that would have been unthinkable fifteen years ago, even though much of the theoretical literature employed is much older than this, as the recent explorations of the work of Henri Bergson in the context of feminist theory testify (Grosz, 2004; 2005). What gives this literature its newness is how it reads now, and, I would argue, not least in a context where it is presented as a critique of the concept of performativity as it has come to be understood in feminist and cultural theory. This is the intriguing dynamic I wish to explore here. How does this work bear upon feminist theory's espousal of performativity? How do materiality, creativity and 'life' come to be posited as an exposure of performativity's analytic fallacy? And what is the importance of acknowledging the context – or 'environment' – where the debate becomes 'localized' or territorialized (for example, within feminist theory)?

Some of this critical direction results from an engagement with the thought of Gilles Deleuze and Félix Guattari. Thus one finds feminist theorist Rosi Braidotti aligning herself with Deleuzean thought because she finds there support for a project of feminism inspired by 'radical immanence' centred on 'embodied materialism' (2002: 5). This she clearly regards as an alternative to performativity, which she criticizes, inter alia, for its 'Derridean' notion of repetition whereby the 'violence of the signifier' returns (Braidotti, 2002: 42, 52) with each citation, as well as for the Hegelian 'shadow' she finds cast over the work of Judith Butler (Braidotti 2002: 42). By contrast, Braidotti is inspired principally by the notion of 'becoming' not least, it seems, because this notion departs from the necessity to posit identity as consciousness, allowing a broader consideration of identifications as processes – material, partial and radically situated processes – arguments to which we will return below.

The influence of Bergson, too, might be traced on the one hand to Deleuze's interest in his thought (1988/1966). Thus Elizabeth Grosz's theoretical project has seen her move from an engagement with Deleuze to an exploration of Bergson, read in her recent work in relation to Darwin and Nietzsche, and thus in relation to notions of time and evolution (2004; 2005).

On the other hand, however, this interest is not only the mining of an intellectual's theoretical trajectory, for much of the impetus comes from the contemporary world where developments in scientific work – in chemistry and biotechnology, but also in relation to physics – are prompting reconsiderations of the nature of 'matter' and of 'life'. This eye to contemporary scientific and medical developments gives the challenge to performativity a focus other than disagreement at the level of theory, which can appear to arise from mere difference of opinion. Thus Vicki Kirby's (1997) critique of performativity is made principally on the level of theory, a critique of the way a notion of 'matter' in Judith Butler's work is something that has to be written *on* by 'the social' or 'culture'. Whenever she turns to matter, Butler returns to it with the understanding that '[to] return to matter requires that we return to matter as a sign' (1993: 49), so that although she 'doesn't dispute the existence of a world before or without language', writes Kirby, 'its unmediated substantiveness remains unthinkable and unrepresentable' (1997: 109); in this way the *substance* of nature is consequently placed under erasure (1997: 114, 125). But Kirby is also asserting her alternative position with reference to developments in physics – specifically the confirmation of the EPR (Epstein, Podolsky and Rosen) thesis in 1982 (Davies and Gribbin, 1992) – that have altered understandings of how information is communicated such that 'it seems that the universe is so thoroughly in touch with itself on the atomic level that information, if I can call it that, in its nonlocal ubiquity, is generalised' (1997: 113). While matter, for Butler, is unintelligible to itself (humans being the sole possessors of language), Kirby suggests that if 'data is received before it is sent' (1997: 113–14) perhaps matter, or as she would prefer it to be termed, *substance*, is 'considerably more articulate' (1997: 114) than accounts of performativity à la Butler have allowed (see also Cheah, 1996; Fraser, 2002).

Elsewhere, the theorization of performative processes in clinical and pharmaceutical contexts has concluded that while the concept of performativity proclaims the necessity to recognize the technical operations that bring about the *seemingly* pre-discursive nature of matter, the concept, *as a radical intervention,* rests upon the sense that 'bodies do not, "in fact", accord with their investiture'[1] (Rosengarten, 2004: 17), and this discordance – this 'more than' – is, moreover, crucial to comprehend the processes at work in such settings. Marsha Rosengarten argues that 'viral resistance', as it is understood in the HIV clinic, is a measurement produced under specific conditions, requiring the intervention of drugs and of (viral load) testing; but 'there is more taking place in the field of HIV than an account of the intra-activity of the observing process tells us' (Rosengarten, 2004: 16). There is in the seeming capacity of matter to 'un-do itself' (Keane and Rosengarten, 2002) – as expressed in the notion of viral resistance (in the presence of drugs) and the virus's re-becoming 'wild type' – the 'palpable presence of matter' in so far as these processes indicate matter that is 'in excess of an investiture enacted through the reiterative process' (Rosengarten, 2004: 17).

Central to the critique of performativity, then, is the activity, indeed the self-organization of matter, that is, the possibility of its creativity beyond the operations of anything we could understand as 'the cultural'. On this point, the impact of the work of Ilya Prigogine and Isabelle Stengers (1984) (see also Prigogine, 1997), to which we shall return below, has been considerable. Again, the concern here is with the creativity of matter, and specifically the study of situations in which matter can be said to 'choose' its solution to a situation. Describing far-from-equilibrium situations in the field of thermodynamics, Prigogine writes, 'matter acquires new properties when far from equilibrium in that fluctuations and instabilities are now the norm. Matter becomes more "active"' (1997: 65). His commentary is explicit about the implications that new developments in comprehending scientific processes might have for the way we think about our world, of profound interest not least because Prigogine regards them as lending support to the emphasis on creativity in the philosophical work of both Whitehead and Bergson (1997: 72).[2]

Performativity is challenged on many counts, then, but they circle around what emerges as a central issue: how to understand the self-activity and creativity of the material world. The material world here includes the matter of the body, but this debate is now reaching beyond the 'language versus the material body' dimensions it adopted in the mid-1990s. The implications are wide and deep. Elizabeth Grosz writes in the introduction to her recent book:

This book functions primarily as a reminder to social, political and cultural theorists, particularly those interested in feminism, antiracism and questions of the politics of globalization, that they have forgotten a crucial dimension of research ... not just the body, but that which makes possible and limits its actions: the precarious, accidental, contingent, expedient, striving, dynamic status of *life in a messy, complicated, resistant, brute world of materiality.* (2004: 2, emphasis added)

Feminist theory has become interested in such questions, then, with these explorations frequently accompanied by claims for a newly reconfigured future for feminist theory. This chapter will seek to comprehend and assess the critique of performativity that this literature presents. With this specific focus in mind, the chapter explores first the move away from Panoptic thinking characterized by Deleuze's developments of Foucault's notion of the '*dispositif*' or apparatus, specifically with an attention to how the emphasis on creativity in Deleuze must be understood as a *critique of coextensivity* as it is understood in the performativity 'paradigm' (see Chapter 1). The second section draws out how creativity emerged from Deleuze's engagement with Bergson's '*elan vital*' and creative evolutionism, so that the importance of the *critique of performativity as preformism* implicit, for example, in the recent work of Grosz, emerges. The third section articulates the challenge to performativity, presenting several points along which there is a divergence between the premises of that concept and the analyses which emphasize processes of self-activity, complexity and life (a 'vital' principle).

Creativity and the Critique of Coextensivity

The notion of performativity as currently deployed within feminist theory refers to the embodiment of normative ideals via a process of mimesis whereby the body is rendered culturally intelligible. The achievement of that cultural intelligibility, then, is simultaneously the production of (gender) difference. Indeed, so well is gender 'indulged' in, in the sense that I described in Chapter 1, that it appears to arise from an interior necessity. But, the argument runs, there is no such interiority by which to comprehend the manifestations of gender, such that the feminist critic's task is to strip the performance of its naturalness or inevitability and to teach us how to see the *exterior* forces of power – the social apparatus – at work in the production of difference. In the ways I have been discussing in previous chapters, difference is something that, in this specific sense, 'exists', as it were, in the regimes of light and enunciation that surround it, more so than it can be said to exist naturally within or between bodies. Or, better, difference emerges as a result of the operations of those regimes that produce it and depend upon their produced elements. In this perspective, as we have seen, difference is only visible and only speakable in so far as we move within certain social apparatuses or *dispositifs* that support it. Thus when Deleuze wrote 'What is a Dispositif?' for a conference on Foucault's work four years after his death, he described the social apparatus or *dispositif* in terms of lines which enable objects to appear and disappear. The apparatus is composed of lines; first and foremost, there are the curves of visibility and curves of enunciation: 'Each apparatus has its way of structuring light, the way it falls, blurs and disperses, distributing the visible and the invisible, giving birth to objects which are dependent on it for their existence, and causing them to disappear.... . If apparatuses have a historical nature, this is to be found in regimes of light, but also in regimes of enunciation' (1992: 160). The distribution of the visible and invisible, and of the sayable and the unsayable, is a consequence of the current organization of the *dispositif* within which objects appear. The production of difference emerges from that organization, from the discursive and non-discursive organization of the domain in question, where non-discursive refers principally, as in the Panoptic situation, to architectural organization of space and light and the institutional organization of time and motion. To focus on the object or to enquire of the nature of difference, then, is to focus too narrowly; rather, one has always to follow the curves to reveal the constitutive forces that animate the scene, that constitute the object and its contemporary intelligibility.

However, in the context of this chapter's task to understand the specificities of the contemporary critique of performativity, it is important to hear how in the piece 'What is a Dispositif?', as well as in his book *Foucault* (1988/1986), Deleuze's sympathetic account of his friend's philosophy nevertheless develops a mode of thinking that is clearly in tension with Foucauldian analyses.

Let us begin with the mantra we have been discussing throughout: no interiority, but only ever *coextensivity*. Recall how, as Deleuze puts it, Foucault's ship is a fold of the sea (Deleuze, 1988/1986: 97), the seeming integrity of the object a product of the workings of the *dispositif*, of the lines of light and enunciation that have that object as their mobile, incomplete product. So difference – such as sexual difference – is understood as indicative of the implicit or explicit power, even violence, of the regime within which it appears, such that what is readable on the body is only ever the embodiment, momentary if repeated to the point of seeming sedimentary, of forces that emanate from without. The sustenance of the element in question by this external process is what allows for the achievement of difference.

As Deleuze reads Foucault's oeuvre, he finds the recurrent theme of the fold. From *Madness and Civilization* through to the later volumes of the *History of Sexuality*, he reads from one book to another, gradually building his own reading, the Deleuzean reading of Foucault, in which the subjectification process is figured as a process of folding. He follows the 'games of repetition' (1988/1986: 98), whereby Foucault 'is always concerned with showing how the Other, the Distant, is also the Near and the Same', as Foucault put it in *Madness and Civilization*, which in Deleuze's words becomes figured as the fold: 'it resembles exactly the invagination of a tissue in embryology, or the act of doubling in sewing: twist, fold, stop and so on' (1988/1986: 98). Through Foucault's interest in Raymond Roussel and the notion of the 'snag' – 'no longer the accident of tissue but the new rule on the basis of which the external tissue is twisted, invaginated and doubled' (1988/1986: 98) – to Foucault's final works where he explores notions such as *enkrateia,* a sort of self-mastery, a mastery over the inside which becomes 'hollowed out' as a relation with the self is allowed to emerge and that can be understood as the Greek version of the snag and the doubling, Deleuze follows this theme's locus.

But Deleuze's reading of Foucault continues in such a way as to hint at his own thinking, and the subtle difference between Foucault and himself. According to Deleuze's reading, in *The History of Sexuality Volume Two: The Use of Pleasure* Foucault suggested that the folding does have the possibility of establishing a subjectivity which, while of course derived from power and knowledge, is not dependent upon them (1988/1986: 101): '[The line of sub-jectivication] is a line of escape. It escapes preceding lines and *escapes from itself*' (1992: 161, emphasis added). In other words, subjectivity, as Foucault comes to regard it through the texts studied in *The Use of Pleasure,* breaks off from the lines of force which brought it into being and establishes a relation to self; in the practice of the relation to the self, there is what Deleuze would call a line of escape or flight by which one establishes one's subjectivity (1988/1986: 102). At this point in his account, so too does Deleuze's writing break away, circling as he moves beyond admiration to emphasize a certain reading as he circles Foucault's thematic in order to produce something which amounts to his own argument.

This notion of the line of escape which may continue preceding lines but then loops and forms new shapes and spaces such that it breaks from them, is a reading of Foucault that belongs very much to a Deleuzean reading. Indeed, Deleuze's reading of the *dispositif* or apparatus draws it close to his own notion of the assemblage. The 'lines' encircle and seem to give rise to objects and sub-jects; but for Deleuze coextensivity does not mean an imposition of an interiority from outside. Rather coextensivity would be another term to describe the rhi-zomatic nature of the lines of Foucault's *dispositif*: 'These apparatuses, then, are composed of the following elements: lines of visibility and enunciation, lines of force, lines of subjectification, lines of splitting, breakage, fracture, all of which criss-cross and mingle together, some lines reproducing and giving rise to others, by means of variations or even changes in the way they are grouped' (1992: 162). The assemblage is made up of the extensions, therefore, that extend ex-periences and carry the situatedness of any point away from itself, connecting it to many other points. If desire connects the baby to the breast, an extension that takes that relationship beyond the question of nourishment and into a realm of fantasy, the line that is drawn (out) between the infant and breast means that as the breast becomes more than it actually 'is'.[3] The line traces a process of deter-ritorialization, and begins to produce a movement, an arrangement. The arrangement is then captured, as the molecular is 'captured' by the molar, or as the micro-political is 'over-coded' by the big binaries of political machines (see Deleuze and Parnet, 2002/1997), so that there – at least potentially – arises a social machine, 'the family' let's say. Such a social machine cannot be studied from the point of view of the state or the contractual relationships that make it up. As Deleuze put it, the analytic task is to follow the tangled paths of the assemblage: 'We have as many tangled lines as a hand … What we [Deleuze and Guattari] call by different names – schizo-analysis, micro-politics, pragmatics, diagrammatism, rhizomatics, cartography – has no other object than the study of these lines, in groups or as individuals' (2002/1977: 125). Amidst these paths will be those of the 'line of flight … of the greatest gradient': 'this line appears to arise [*surgir*] afterwards, to become detached from the two others, if indeed it succeeds in detaching itself' (2002/1977: 125). This line of flight is a movement of creativity within the tangle of lines of the *dispositif*.

What is at stake here is how one understands this creativity. For this creativity does not seemingly replace or contradict coextensivity in Deleuze's understanding. There are still lines of light, knowledge, power and subjectification that encircle and produce the effect of interiorities. These must remain in our analysis. But it certainly means that for Deleuze and Guattari following movements of becoming – or, to anticipate a Bergsonian language, attempting to trace the path by which a differing, a specific becoming, is actualized – is also to trace the path of desire,[4] of a creativity which, in so far as it can be posited as a relationship of the thing to itself, as much as a relation between points of stillness and seeming unity, implies a version of interiority and a critique of the mantra 'no interiority, only coextensivity'. What has been, if not denied, then bracketed, namely the creativity of things, their self-activity, indeed, the very insistence of *life*, is put back into the frame.

This is an important challenge to the notion of coextensivity as it has been employed in so much cultural theory, wherever Foucault's *dispositif* is taken as an account of how difference exists fundamentally outside the subject, only coming to life, as it were, in the fold of the subject. Versions of this process of enfolding are implied wherever difference is understood as produced 'discursively' (and this may be more often in the criticism of the argument than in the argument itself), or wherever difference is presented, for example, as the result of the violence of the category. In Deleuze's reading of Foucault and in his own arguments (both alone and with Guattari), however, another perspective emerges. To be clear: in this approach to the apparatus, difference is not posited as if it were only ever the product or resultant, imposed *by* the apparatus. Difference is not to be understood as an imposition of a distinction that exists in the regimes of light and enunciation, in the *dispositif*, still less a *citation* of a difference located within discourse, because, in senses to be explored further below, difference is the name given to movement itself: difference is the very motor of creativity.

There is here a very different energy gleaned from Foucault's work, an immanent force that makes it impossible to understand difference as solely the enfolding of an external categorization, an order(ing) from without.[5] To understanding the 'carrying on' of difference as the embodiment of an imposed order, or as a strategy enacted for cultural survival, is to under-emphasize the sense in which the embodied *lives*. And this is not to imply, as many have in relation to Judith Butler's thesis, that the body imposes a material limit on the possibilities of discursive manipulation as if this were to be understood as the 'discourse versus the material body' debate. But it is an elaboration of Panoptical thinking that takes analysis on a very different tack, for it is to suggest that there is a self-activity of differing, that the – any – body's movements and attractions are such that it has a creative responsiveness and mobility not only within the lines of the dispositifs within which it is sustained (or not) *but also with itself*. This is a crucial shift in emphasis. Here the embodied subject moves such that, as Gutting remarks, 'a being, simply as a being, is a locus of the heterogeneity (novelty, creativity) that is difference.' (2001: 336) Difference, then, must be understood as *what being is in itself*, not (only) how it is related to other things, and the repetition of a being, its con-tinued existence through time or every new instantiation of it, can only be an expression of this heterogeneity. The next section pursues this argument further, again with its attention focused on understanding where this line of thought poses its challenge to performativity.

Differentiation and/as Life: The Critique of Preformism

In Deleuze's view, it is with heterogeneity that one must begin. His thought develops out of two 'intuitions' (in Bergson's sense of the term): first, that being is radically diverse, and secondly, that correspondingly, thought is a recognition of ontological diversity, not a reduction to unity (Gutting, 2001: 332). Where historically philosophy has privileged unity, Deleuze rejects the necessity of the assumption that matter must imitate form. This leads him to a conception of difference that could not be reconciled with the taking up of an ideal or the approximation of a norm as implied wherever a process of imi-tation or citation is posited. For reasons that will become clear, these two con-cepts are recast.[6]

Classical metaphysics enquired of the ontological status of form and matter and the relation between the two: Do forms exist independently of matter, as in the Platonic notion of ideal forms, so that matter 'imitates' forms? Or, as for Aristotle, do forms not exist separately but work instead only as principles of structure for matter? Traditional metaphysics privileges unity of forms, making it the basis and explanation of differences. Differences in kind occur because one kind includes forms that another does not; differences within kinds occur because forms belong to different sub-kinds. In this way, forms determine reality (difference) so that difference is always derived from unified metaphysical

structures (Gutting, 2001: 335). To understand Deleuze's philosophical challenge, one has to understand his thought as an objection to the assumption that
there are such principles of unity. Why, his philosophy asks, should we begin
with the assumption of forms, whatever their ontological status? Rather than a
belief in unified and unifying structures, could we not begin with a belief in difference as the fundamental principle and differing as the ontological assumption? Here is the decisive influence of Henri Bergson on Deleuze. As he argues
in 'La conception de la différence chez Bergson', his ontological project is to
pursue the Bergsonian thought that 'the thing differs from itself, *in the first place,
immediately*' (1999: 53).

As Michael Hardt points out, Deleuze reads Bergson as a polemic against
dominant philosophical tradition, and most especially against Hegelian
thought with its 'negative logic of being'. For Hegel – himself arguing against
Spinoza's positive being – being has to differentiate itself from nothingness.
Being has to involve negation in the sense of differentiating itself from what is
other than itself, both passively and actively. There is a negative logic at work
here because for Hegel nothing exists without this negative movement away
from something else. For Deleuze, to see the necessity of being based in
negated difference in this way is to locate the necessity of being as *exterior* to
being. Importantly, Deleuze argues that a cause that remains external to its
effect cannot be *necessary* since, to simplify here, the being had to exist prior
to the exterior 'cause' in order for the latter to be understood as exterior. An
external cause can only sustain the *possibility* of being, whereas for being to be
necessary, *the fundamental ontological cause must be internal* to its effect.[7]
Bergson's thought is attractive to Deleuze in part because he aids in this anti-
Hegelian task; Bergson allows Deleuze to argue that what grounds being is
movement, an internal, vital movement he terms 'difference'. Thus although
'difference' is the key term for Deleuze, it is not understood in Hegelian
fashion. It 'does not refer to a static contrast of qualities in real being; rather,
difference marks the real dynamic of being – it is the movement that grounds
being' (Hardt, 1993: 2). Deleuze

> gives difference a radically new role. Difference founds being; it provides being with
> its necessity, its substantiality. We cannot understand this argument for internal differ-
> ence over external difference unless we recognise the ontologically fundamental role
> that difference is required to fill. (Hardt, 1993: 5)

Difference is the internal motor of being, which, as we shall see, does not mean
that it *determines* being. In Hardt's neat formulation, one has to enquire as to
how difference sustains its being, rather than, as Hegelian logic would have it,
how being sustains its difference. In short, 'difference' for Deleuze must be
understood as a question of what being is in itself, not solely how it is related
to other things. Thus the remark quoted above – 'a being, simply as a being,

is a locus of the heterogeneity (novelty, creativity) that *is* difference' (Gutting, 2001: 336, italics added) – has a critical force because it asserts a dynamic *both positive and interior* where critical thought has become so habituated to negativity and movements in relation to external forces.

In its first 'intuitions', then, Deleuzean thought departs from any inheritance of Hegelian thought that would regard difference as established via an oppositional, negating movement. Moreover, because difference is understood as a matter of what being is in itself, and not how it is related to other things, differentiation is a – indeed, the – *vital* process. This Bergsonian *élan vital* animates being; its process of differentiation is the basic movement of life. Deleuze writes in *Bergsonism*: 'What does Bergson mean when he talks about *élan vital?* It is always a case of a virtuality in the process of being actualized, a simplicity in the process of differentiating, a totality in the process of dividing. Proceeding "by dissociation and division," by "dichotomy," is the essence of life' (1988/1966: 94).[8]

For our task here, the crux is how this process is understood. For Bergson, 'differentiation is never a negation but a creation, and difference is never negative but essentially positive and creative' (Deleuze, 1988/1966: 103). Importantly, the emphasis on creativity is to be read as a bar on any analysis that would proceed from an understanding of a process of realization as guided by *resemblance* and *limitation*. If we understand difference as the 'miming of hegemonic ideals' (Butler, 1993: 125), for example, there is an implication that the process at stake is the realization in matter (or what Butler termed in that text the 'materialization' or 'sedimentation' (1993: 15)) of that which resembles something dictated in the realm of the intelligible or the possible, that is, in the realm of possibilities that Butler argues is currently arranged so as to foreclose our possibilities of becoming otherwise, but that has – this is the basis for political hope – the potential to be expanded. From this point of view, the real is thought to be the image of, or to resemble, the possible that it realizes. The real 'simply has reality added to it … [so that] from the point of view of the concept there is no difference between the possible and the real' (Deleuze 1988/1966: 97). Here, existence becomes a mere quality or attribute (Grosz, 2004: 187). Moreover, the process of realization must proceed by limitation, since the realm of the possible is much wider than the realm of the real. But if everything is pre-given in the realm of the possible, the argument runs, the passage of realization is not a creation; it is what amounts to a sort of *preformism*. And this would be one of the main charges that underlies the critique of performativity arising from this work. That is, performativity is *preform*ativity wherever analysis claims to describe the idea(l)-form that the subject is said to imitate or instantiate.

The alternative process that Deleuze posits through his reading of Bergson is a process of actualization guided by difference and creation. Rather than a realm of the possible (and the real), one has virtuality (and actualization). Rather than resemblance and limitation, one has creative differentiation. From this alternative perspective, 'Virtuality exists in such a way that it is realised in dissociating itself, that it is forced to dissociate itself in order to realise itself. Differentiation is the movement of a virtuality that is actualising itself' (Deleuze, 1999: 93).

The process of differentiation is creative because in order for the virtual to become actual it must create its own terms of actualization. As Deleuze emphasizes, *the actual does not resemble the virtuality that it embodies* (1988/1966: 97). There is no resemblance, there is no dictation of its form; rather there is a creative evolution, an original production of the multiplicity of actual being through differentiation.[9] This is preferable, Deleuze explains, because otherwise there is a sleight of hand at work:

> If the real is said to resemble the possible, is this not in fact because the real was expected to come about by its own means, to "project backward" a fictitious image of it, and to claim that it was possible at any time, before it happened? In fact, it is not the real that resembles the possible, it is the possible that resembles the real, because it has been abstracted from the real once made, arbitrarily extracted from the real like a sterile double. Hence, we no longer understand anything either of the mechanism of difference or of the mechanism of creation. (1988/1966: 98)

For Bergson, actualization names this mechanism of creation. Actualization is a differentiation by which heterogeneous lines of actualization diverge from a virtual unity. As Elizabeth Grosz describes it, in ways that hint at the implications she finds for feminist and radical movements, the movement of actualization is 'the opening up of the virtual to what befalls it. It is fundamentally unpredictable, innovative' (2004: 189). This is, of course, tied up with Bergson's arguments regarding evolution, as Deleuze glosses it:

> Evolution takes place from the virtual to actuals. Evolution is actualization, actualization is creation... . [C]ontrary to preformism, evolutionism will always have the merit of reminding us that life is production, creation of differences. (1988/1966: 98)

The importance of evolution in Bergson's arguments regarding the virtual and the actual is crucial. Grosz suggests that one might read Bergson's *Creative Mind* as an elaboration of Darwin's understanding of individual variation along the lines of Nietzsche's will to power:

> Instead of regarding evolutionary fitness as the passive adaptation to the active effects of the environment, Bergson sees life as an active, excessive, inventive response to the provocation or stimulus of the environment, which induces in life, not just adequate

or bare adaptation, but the capacity for immense – indeed excessive – development, elaboration, and complication. (2004: 200, drawing on *Creative Mind*)

Bergson insisted on the dynamic nature of evolution, its creativity. Evolution is a process of differentiation that has to be understood as mobile and open-ended; life is the continual differentiation, the production of the multiple variations that are provoked as life 'rises to the provocations that the environment, including other species, poses to each individual and species' (Grosz, 2004: 206, paraphrasing Bergson). Bergson regarded his task as treading a path between the 'hypothesis of purely accidental variation [mechanism] and that of a variation directed in a definite way under the influence of external conditions [finalism]' (Bergson, 1911: 62, in Grosz 2004: 207). His position, as Grosz explains, developed through a discussion of evolutionary convergence, that is, the development of similar organs – the eye is a key example – in a range of vastly different species.

Bergson's argument is that the greater the divergence of lines of evolutionary development the more unlikely it is that a complex organ such as the eye would be prompted to develop in two species by variations resulting from accidental influences, whether inner or outer (Bergson, 1911: 54, in Grosz 2004: 207). Convergent development leads him to argue that there must be a common progenitor, whose offspring diverged further and further apart yet still retain 'some trace, rudimentary or developed, of their common origin' (Grosz, 2004: 207). While one may never know this common origin from studying the divergent paths of its evolution, one may believe that 'even in the latest channel there would be something of the impulsion received at source' (Bergson, 1911: 54, quoted in Grosz 2004: 207). In other words, variations are actualized along such lines that something of the (virtual) unity remains. Deleuze stresses the importance of this point: 'evolution does not move from one actual term to another actual term in a homogeneous unilinear series, but *from a virtual term to the heterogeneous terms that actualise it* along a ramified series' (1988/1966: 100, emphasis added).

Thus Bergson argued that *élan vital* is a process of differentiation, division and bifurcation; life is not passive adaptation to the activity of the external environment but is itself an active response, a differentiation – *not* an addition, association or augmentation – producing the divergence of evolutionary lines and the differences in kind which we witness at any given time. Life rises to the provocations of the environment; through the self-activity, the differentiation, variation ensues.

Performativity Challenged?

There is much that is, both initially and ultimately, shared between the concept of performativity and the perspectives that are beginning to emerge for feminist theory within this work, more than is often acknowledged. This is unsurprising, perhaps, given the to some extent shared intellectual trajectory exemplified not only in the close and respectful relationship between Foucault and Deleuze, but also in the shared genealogical impulse that nevertheless takes its different routes from Nietzsche. Bergson, for his part, shared the crucial emphasis on radical contingency (see Ansell Pearson footnote 60, 1999: 165) and a critique of teleological thought, central in feminist work on performativity. Thus Grosz's conclusions for feminism, after her reading of Bergson (2004: 259–61), often sound as if, in terms of their political hopes, they might have been penned by Judith Butler: 'At their most critical and incisive, such [feminist and queer] struggles aim for a future in which the sexes are no longer recognizable in their present terms, in which sexuality and sexual pleasure have been redefined beyond their current divisions, categories and activities, in which identity is seen in terms of what is to come rather than what has been ...' (2004: 261). Likewise, and perhaps because there is much that is at peace between Foucault and Deleuze, the distance between Braidotti and Butler seems at times needlessly exaggerated given the feminist positions they both wish to further. Nevertheless, it would be churlish to deny that there is also much that is under contention. The following will spell out, with many ifs and buts, the most important aspects of the critique of performativity emerging here.

First, as mentioned above, one of the most important aspects of the critique is the contrast between the positivity one finds in Bergson and Deleuze and the negative critical tradition that comes from the Hegelian line. The fundamentally different premise of the traditions – the one emanating from the positive impulse of *élan vital*, the other from the negative movement of the dialectic – gives the different critical stance of say, Braidotti and Butler (see Butler, 2004a: 198), or more clearly, between the work of Grosz and Butler. In the one there is difference because life will result in difference; life *is* differentiation, a creative positive force. In the other, difference emerges as a struggle of the thing against all that it is not; it is an achievement, a result of cultural arrangements within which the elements are sociopolitically, and antagonistically, placed. Writes Deleuze: 'Alteration must maintain itself and find its status without letting itself be reduced to plurality, or even to contradiction, or to alterity even. This is where the Bergsonian theory and method of difference is opposed to that other method, to that other theory of difference that is called the dialectic, as much Plato's dialectic of alterity as Hegel's dialectic of contradiction, both implying the power and presence of the negative' (1999: 49).

Of course it might be objected that this distinction between positivity and negativity simplifies the contrast between these two approaches. There is in Bergson not just differentiation as life, but the concern with how difference is understood and the relations between emergent entities. Furthermore, one might read the 'performativity paradigm' as containing more Deleuzean 'positive' impulses than are readily apparent, as many have. In Judith Butler's work the influence of Spinoza remains, so that one finds the 'desire to exist' – and to exist well, that is, ethically – giving a positive force to the individual's continued existence (in *The Psychic Life of Power*, for example, where Butler writes 'the desire to survive, "to be", is a pervasively exploitable desire' (1997b: 7) or in a recent conference paper, 2003). But this desire to exist is posited because it is 'endlessly exploitable', because it explains the individual's attachment to the power relations that constitute its being (1997b) – and thus to emphasize once again the presence of a negative, if dialectically productive, force – rather than as the impulse to actualization that it might become in the Bergson realm.

Secondly, a related point, the assertion of interiority that comes with the emphasis on creativity and the self-activity of living things flies in the face of performativity's premise. Where this interiority is understood as a prompting of processes of actualization or as the movement from the virtual to the actual, and hence as a critique of preformism, it might also be read as a critique of performativity in so far as the latter can be presented as preformism. That is, if the *dispositif* operates through limitation and resemblance – for example, where difference is understood to result from the citation of a category division (pre-)existent within discourse – it infers the realm of the possible from that of the real.

Another way of making this same point is to say that the theory of performativity accords the apparatus too much, or, better, to avoid the dichotomy that way of speaking erroneously sets up, that it cannot account for moments when the self-activity of matter, of its self-organization and reorganization implies (other, additional) creative processes of life. In other words, the notion that there is no interiority, no 'doer behind the deed' should not imply that there is *only* human speech and action; without reintroducing 'the subject' as agent, one can admit all sorts of other processes and lines of movement that intercept, run parallel and encircle deeds and their trajectories, limiting and enabling them. This is one point of entry for Brian Massumi's (2002) argument in so far as he insists that the 'self-activity of experience' – in this instance the experience of colour – has the ability to display 'a self-insistent dynamism that commends itself to the instituted context, into which it breaks and enters' (2002: 220). This ingressive activity of experience is not the property of language acts or the language users but it *enters* their situation and becomes personalized there. The regularizations of discourse and institutions make the processual openness and self-activity of the world recede (2002: 220); but the self-activity of the world is a real, material reserve of unpredictable potential: 'reality is an ... inexhaustible reserve of surprise' which, when it enters a situation, indicates 'the presence of process' (2002: 226).

If processes in the world can self-organize and emerge so as to surprise us, such that matter cannot be said to imitate forms according to laws – for that

'model leaves many things, active and affective, by the wayside' (Deleuze and
Guattari, 1988: 408) – the operations of a social apparatus of normalization
cannot be considered to constitute matter, nor to control the processes at
stake. Hence the excitement of Prigogine (1997) and Prigogine and Stengers'
(1984) work on far-from-equilibrium situations (which has fuelled the rise of
the concept of complexity and has drawn the attention, inter alia, of sociologists, see especially Hayles, 1990, 1999; Urry and Law, 2004; Urry, 2005).
Prigogine explains that his work on far-from-equilibrium systems suggests that
at a critical distance from equilibrium, unlike what happens at equilibrium,
systems do not conform to principles of free energy or entropy production.
Fluctuations and instabilities occur as new processes set in and increase the
production of entropy (1997: 65–7). 'In short, distance from equilibrium
becomes an essential parameter in describing nature much like temperature in
equilibrium thermodynamics' (1997: 68). At the bifurcation point, matter
acquires new properties, abandoning the universal laws of nature valid at equilibrium. Prigogine gives the example of the Belousov-Zhabotinski reaction – a
'spectacular example of chemical oscillation':

> I remember our amazement when we saw the reacting solution become blue, and then
> red, and then blue again. Today many other oscillatory reactions are known ... but the
> B-Z reactions ... proved that matter far from equilibrium acquires new properties.
> Billions of molecules become simultaneously blue, then red. This entails the appear-
> ance of long-range correlations in far from equilibrium conditions that are absent in a
> state of equilibrium. Again, we can say that matter at equilibrium is 'blind', but far
> from equilibrium it begins to 'see'. (1997: 67)

The system's oscillating and 'choosing' among different solutions allows
Prigogine to speak of matter having 'sight'. Nothing in the macroscopic equa-
tions justifies the preference for any one solution (1997: 68) and even if the
initial values and boundary constraints are known, there are still many states
available to the system among which it chooses as a result of fluctuations (1997:
70). 'Once we have dissipative structures, we can speak of self-organisation,'
writes Prigogine (1997: 70). Or again, Stengers and Prigogine suggest that at
this point of instability we might say that matter can 'see': 'we have recently discovered a striking example of the fundamental new properties that matter
acquires in far-from-equilibrium conditions; external fields such as the gravita-
tional field can be "perceived" by the system, creating the possibility of pattern
selection' (1984: 163). That is, in non-equilibrium situations the effect of grav-
itation is magnified.
    Speaking of the simplest scenario in which two stable solutions present
themselves in the non-equilibrium situation (creating a 'pitchfork bifurcation'), Prigogine suggests that the solution can be understood as the manifestation of 'intrinsic differentiation between parts of the system itself and the

system and its environment' (1997: 69). Here the link to the work of Bergson – actualization is a differentiation by which heterogeneous lines of actualization diverge from a virtual unity – as well as Whitehead's emphasis on the 'creativity of nature', becomes apparent, a link of which Prigogine was well aware.

For our purposes here, the assertion of interiority, or 'self-organization', is important because it appears to challenge the emphasis on language or cultural processes as constitutive of difference. Thus Butler's argument that 'the process of that sedimentation or what we might call materialization will be a kind of citationality, the acquisition of being through the citing of power' (1993: 15), or that the production of gender difference as a result of 'the miming of hegemonic ideals' (1993: 125) has been criticized for its giving up of materiality to language, for its reduction of matter to the non-articulate (Kirby, 1997; see also Barad, 2003). The questions of how matter itself communicates, and how life differentiates itself, are profound questions that simply cannot be posed when the emphasis is on 'performativity'.

However, the force and objective of this argument, when presented as a criticism of performativity, is not always properly formulated. Thus Kirby's critique of Butler seems to miss the thrust of Butler's work. Butler has never claimed to have a theory of matter exactly; her attention has always been on the social operations of power that – as we know only too well from the continued practice of racism in the face of DNA – can override whatever is occurring at the level of 'material' systems. Butler has always admitted that her efforts to attend to the material have led her back toward the discursive – 'I've never been a good materialist' she wrote recently in part in response to Braidotti, 'Every time I try to write about the body, the writing ends up being about langauage' (2004a: 198). But her notion of the discursive is more than language – performativity involves more than speech, including bodily acts – such that the pitch of Kirby's interventions are sometimes too specifically tied there. Moreover, there is a sense in which Kirby's forthright critique of Butler seems to 'forget' the context or *environment* within which the debate has been staged.

The recent work of Anne Marie Mol (2002) constitutes a wonderful example of how attending to the materiality and organic processes of the body *does not remove* but complicates the need for questions in relation to the constitution of interiority by social processes and technologies; these questions must remain within the analysis. The relation between what 'is' and how the 'is' is enacted and 'revealed' require critical scrutiny. In her study of the processes by which 'atherosclerosis' – the thickening and gradual obstruction of the arteries – is diagnosed and treated, Mol attends to the coordinated practices of the patient's accounts, doctor's assessments and laboratory test results. When the procedures and their attendant technologies agree, the notion that there is a single disease residing in the body seems obvious. The stenosis causes the pain that the patient reports, it causes the pressure loss (the difference between blood pressure in the arms and the ankles) measured by the technician's instruments, and it causes the darkening on the X-ray images that will guide the surgeon's procedure if surgery is recommended. When these practices disagree, however, a series of balancing tasks, calculations, decisions and adjudications take place in which the possibility of referring to an internal, causal, pre-existing reality is not possible as a guide to further treatment. One patient's test results suggest he should be in pain, but he arrives on a motorbike reporting minimal pain; another patient reports pain on walking but his blood pressure results are within the normal range. Mol argues that it is not the case that there is a simple hierarchy in which, say, the most technical of the procedures will automatically win out over the others. Contradictions *may* lead to one fact being given more weight than another, but the positions in that hierarchy are not set in advance (2002: 53–66). Certainly any 'interior/exterior' distinction is unhelpful here. For Mol, the body has to be understood not as fragmented, but as multiply produced by these techniques and procedures. Disease is not merely about interpretation, but it is a complex process of coordinated enactment.

It is debatable whether Mol's work is a critique of performativity or an extension of it; all would depend upon the understanding one had of the concept of performativity and its boundaries. Nevertheless, the point I would wish to make here, and thirdly, is that these challenges suggest the need to attend more closely and more broadly, to the relationship between interiority and *environment*. The presence of 'interior' process does not eliminate the importance of the external environment. Far from it: in Bergson the process at stake is precisely the organism's relation to the environment, the elaboration of the environment's stimulus. And as we have seen, in Prigogine and Stengers' work, the 'perception' of the environment enters the resolution of instability. Elsewhere, Isabelle Stengers has emphasized the importance of attending to what she reminds us Whitehead nicely referred to as the '*patience of the environment*' (Stengers, 2001, 13). That is, the ways the etho-ecological regime in which an organism is sustained allows it so to do (or not). Stengers writes:

> For Whitehead the ethos of an organism, its specific grasping together of aspects of its environment, cannot be dissociated from its ecology, that is from the way other organisms prehend and grasp together aspects of this organism, including the way they are themselves prehended and grasped by it. Each organism thus depends on what Whitehead calls the 'patience of the environment'. The possibility for the environment not to be patient may easily be exemplified by many human interactions. It is well known that people are unable to keep talking if the one they address listens without blinking, a human ethological sign meaning 'yes I am listening'. And we can also think about the collective dynamics of uncontrollable laughter in order to understand why

Whitehead uses the beautiful word 'infection' to describe the etho-ecological regime of reciprocal prehensions. (2001: 13)

These arguments move us then, beyond the discourse, power and spatial choreography of Panoptical thinking into a consideration of the environment that sustains the organism in an etho-ecological sense, *and which it 'grasps'*. The critique of performativity here is that it needs to expand its considerations to consider how performances necessarily take place within other sorts of etho-ecological assemblages. And while work such as Kelly Oliver's (2001) on 'air' stands as an example of a feminist theorist beginning such explorations, it is important that there cannot be a triumphant finding of the missing or forgotten element, for each situation or event will potentially involve its unique relations, actualizations and modes of sustenance. Indeed, the point is not to set up a debate in which the factors of the environment and the interior are pitted against each other; such a retrogressive step would be a failure to see that the challenge is not just to right the balance between these two factors, but to reconsider the desire for law-like theories itself (Greco, 2005: 23).

Another approach here might be to recast the notion of 'cultural survival' that performativity subtends. As we saw in earlier chapters, cultural survival is a way of comprehending the complicities that the becoming-subject is obliged to enact in order to survive. But if one understands what was referred to there as the cultural context or domain differently, that is, as part of the etho-ecological environment, one begins to address it anew. If the very notion of power relations is rethought with or as virtual/actual relations, the actual has emerged or evolved from the past virtual, and the future will be actualized from the virtual present; but whatever is sustained in the present or will emerge in the future requires that its path be precisely a *sustainable* one, in other words, that its relations with its environment support its emergence, and sustain that becoming. Stengers explains that the etho-ecological points to the 'inseparability of *ethos*, the way of behaving peculiar to a being and *oikos* the habitat of that being and the way it satisfies or opposes the demands associated with the ethos or affords opportunities for an original ethos to risk itself (2005: 997).

This leads us to the fourth challenge to performativity. This would be the de-privileging of the psyche and psychic processes as the site for explanations of the incomplete nature of the subject. Processes Butler might understand psychically, or at least through the language of the psyche, such as the melancholic encrypting Butler describes in *The Psychic Life of Power* (1997b), are understood here in relation to virtuality and evolution. The latent carrying of the other within is less the foreclosed possibility that is culturally disallowed and psychically disavowed, but the dormant within an actualization that carries its (alternative) virtual possibilities with it. Thus writes Grosz: 'Although life itself is a difference in kind from matter, the elevation of matter above its expected expenditure of energy, it is itself divided into mutually exclusive trajectories that nonetheless share a common source *and thus lie dormant within each other*, vegetative or animal, centralized or decentralized nervous system, instinctive or intelligent action, the lines of difference in kind in life itself' (2004: 214, emphasis added). *If, for Butler, the individual emerges due to the attentions of power that enforce an encrypted (im)possibility because heteronormative culture will not support being-otherwise, for Grosz, s/he emerges due to the actualization of a necessarily latent virtuality within an environment that supports that emergence (adaptation).* For both, subjectivity is an achievement that must be placed within its setting, but the lines of extension, contingency, connection, delimitation and support within which the subject comes into being are understood differently.

There is a difference implied in so far as lines of becoming or actualization need not be understood through the lens of a psyche, a conscience or a body. Since subjectivities are the achievement and the site of all kinds of movements of differing and actualization, our interest is refocused on the movement of parts and particles, which is more than a reduction in scale because it is a conceptual change that de-privileges the subject's integrity by noticing the ability of its *qualities* to play with their coextensivity as it were, to travel with aspects and qualities within its environment without a process of psychic identification or dis-identification. The notions of de- and reterritorialization can describe the movement of particles, more properly than, say, peoples. In Deleuze and Guattari's words, it is 'not imitation at all but a capture of code, surplus value of code, an increase in valence, a veritable becoming, a becoming-wasp of the orchid and a becoming-orchid of the wasp' (1988: 10). So, as Jerry Aline Fleiger (2000) points out, the rhizome results from a *material* identification, and a molecular identification, which distinguishes it from the notion of mimesis.[10] Furthermore, the lines of the *dispositif* are multiplied, such that the terms by which Deleuze described Foucault's *dispositif* – 'light', 'enunciation', 'power' and 'subjectification' – no longer suffice; coextensivity becomes the bewildering tangle of multiple lines, all of which are in movement. The lines by which a unit 'extends' beyond 'itself' can be 'travelled', actualized, intensified. To attempt to speak of *a* 'psyche' or *an* 'identity', even as non-essentialist, is to cut into that assemblage of relations to constitute the unit in question, and thereby to cut away other sorts of considerations.

This move to consider the movement of particles in relations of actualization is more, therefore, than the critique of identity as *essentialist* that has long been familiar in feminist and other work, and which is shared by performativity 'paradigm' and these potential challenges to it. Rather, it turns on the possibility of allowing a notion of creativity, even what we might call for short a 'vitalist' order, to be reconsidered. As Monica Greco (2005: 20) has noted, Donna Haraway is often quoted within feminist, cultural and science studies to reinforce an anti-essentialist stance, since she emphasized the *assembly* of objects and persons and discounted the role of 'Nature' as an architect constraining that assembly (or reassembly). She refers, in her *Simians, Cyborgs and Women*, to individuality as a 'strategic defence problem' (1991: 212), which implies that the category of the individual pertains to an order of necessity – a political, or possibly ethical, order (Greco, 2005: 20). But she also implies that the individual is a 'strategic defence problem' in relation to a *vital* order, argues Greco, where for example, she writes in the language of immunology, that: 'disease is a process of misrecognition or transgression of the boundaries of a strategic assemblage called the self' (1991: 212). In Haraway's account, the political ordering of the individual does not therefore *preclude* that the self-assemblage also be understood as an organism. Nor should it, argues Greco, for if the vital order is properly understood, there is no contradiction here, no return to the essentialisms or the teleologies that critics of vitalism have feared. An organism is an unstable system, 'otherwise we would not speak of disease and illness in relation to it' (Greco, personal communication); as Hans Jonas argued, 'nonautarky is the very essence of organism. Its power to use the world, this unique prerogative of life, has its precise reverse in the necessity of *having* to use it, on pain of ceasing to be' (2005: 56, emphasis added). Thus a 'vitalist ontology cannot but be an ontology of the contingent, of what is *permanently suspended* between being and non-being' (Greco, 2005: 20, emphasis added).

Whatever else constitutes the subject, then, because it is also alive, it is a process that sustains itself only in so far as it is sustained by its environment. Organic things have a metabolism by definition, a relationship to matter that sustains them (Jonas, 2005: 55). And precisely because it is 'committed to itself, *put at the mercy of its own performance*, life must depend on conditions over which it has no control and which may deny themselves at any time' (Jonas, 2005: 55). The organic is on the one hand 'emancipated from the identity with matter' yet its survival – until of course its 'ever present contrary, not-being' inevitably overwhelms it – depends, by definition, on matter (2005: 56). That is, Jonas writes, on metabolism: exchanges with matter, taking it in and transiently incorporating it, using it, excreting it (2005: 55).

To recognize this order is not to make obsolete Haraway's other orders – the political, the ethical – nor is it necessarily incompatible with Butler's positing of the complicities in which one's psychic desire to exist results; it is perhaps to assert that these other orders need not occlude analysis of the complicated processes that organic survival is and requires. The forms of assembly and reassembly to which Haraway refers might include the forms of performance dictated by the quest to survive as a living organism, or perhaps one might say, to sustain its own a line of becoming.

The (re-)introduction of the 'vital principle' must not be figured as a paradigm shift. That is, there can be no wielding of the notion of organicism, still less of 'complexity', as if they operated normatively. It would be as suspect to assume self-organization, say, as it would be to refuse its possibility; 'life' does not *replace* 'performance' or 'the social', as Jonas's formulation quoted above implies. As Greco writes, 'complexity' cannot itself be a 'normative operator' or become a source of self-evidence (Greco, 2005: 23–4); but complex situations cannot simply be 'added' to social science or social theoretical endeavours. They are not merely difficult to understand, but throw the very desire for universal laws off course. The aspiration to produce a form of knowledge that is exhaustive and predictive cannot make sense. It is for this reason that triumphalism has no place; any 'vital principle' must be understood as Bergson regarded it, 'a sort of label attached to our ignorance' (1911: 42, quoted in Greco, 2005: 18).

This is not a humility of choice but of necessity. Not only because one cannot see into the future, however much that future is contained within the present – as Grosz writes '[O]ur progeny will differ ... in ways not explained by but already to some extent contained within our present forms' (Grosz, 2004: 214) – but because our interest in understanding processes is not separate from those processes. Greco takes a lead from Stengers, who through her work on complexity, indicates how the term 'expresses a demand that we acknowledge, and learn to value as the source of qualitatively new questions, the possibility of a form of ignorance that cannot be simply deferred to future knowledge. It is the demand that we acknowledge a sensitivity of the world to our interest in it, and to the forms in which this interest is expressed' (Greco, 2005: 25). The notion that our interests in the world enter into the assemblages, affecting them rather than simply reporting on them chimes with the perspectives developed in the last chapter, where I suggested that the genealogist's role might be refigured as part of the ecology, entering into processes of composition. This implies, furthermore, that the 'politics' of analytic frameworks can never be understood as separated from the matters of fact under consideration; they are not added after the results of investigations into 'what is' are known.

Of course, in the philosophy of Deleuze and Guattari and those who work in their vein, there is never a 'gap' across which analysis takes place. In processes of becoming, as described above, or as in *What is Philosophy?* (1994), where they speak of the artwork as a bloc of sensations 'held' in the material, it does not make sense to seek a place from which one observes as if from outside the 'zone of indetermination' or as if outside the artwork.

As percepts, sensations are not perceptions referring to an object (reference): if they resemble something it is with a resemblance produced with their own methods; and the smile on the canvas is made solely with colours, lines, shadow and light. If resemblance haunts the work of art, it is because sensation refers only to its material: it is the percept or affect of the material itself, the smile of oil, the gesture of fired clay, the thrust of metal, the crouch of Romanesque stone, and the ascent of gothic stone. (1994: 167)

Sensations are not to be understood *as* (the) material, however; the point is rather that the material is the condition that preserves the percept or affect: 'so long as the material lasts the sensation enjoys an eternity' (1994: 167). Every time you glance at that portrait, she will smile again. What the artist brings before us is not the resemblance, therefore, but the *sensation* 'of a tortured flower, of a landscape slashed, pressed and plowed' (1994: 167). The aim of art is able to 'extract a bloc of sensations'; style is required to raise perceptions to the percept, affections to the affect (1994: 167) so that 'something' passes from one to the other. This something can only be termed sensation. Between the viewer and the artwork, the reader and the text, there is no gap. There is a becoming rather than a parallel existence: 'We become with the world; we become by contemplating it' (1994: 169).

For them, the role of the critic, philosopher, or political agitator is figured in different ways; but in these various ways, they describe how the assemblage can be made to shudder, even through artworks, or through the use of the minor,[11] or 'style' (1994: 176). The writer makes language 'stammer, tremble, cry or even sing: this is the style, the "Tone", the language of sensations, or the foreign language within language that summons forth a people to come ... The writer twists language, makes it vibrate, seizes hold of it, and rends it in order to wrest the percept from perceptions, the affect from affections, the sensation from opinion – in view, one hopes, of that still missing people' (1994: 176).

Like the creations of the artist, like the perceptions of the film critic,[12] socio-theoretical analyses are not only an evaluation of the world but are also modes of participation in it (see also Urry and Law, 2004, who argue similarly but from a different literature). The question for the theorist is how one's relation to the assemblage is to be understood, a question well beyond the notion that method might act as a prophylactic, as Mariam Fraser nicely puts it, to prevent the contamination of the object or process under investigation (2005: 17).[13] Whether or not one's explicit intention is to make the assemblage stammer and 'sing', if this work converges on any point it would be acknowledgement of the various reverberations that the observer-participant inevitably prompts. Our interest in processes makes us as much a part of them as the reader is of the book, constituted there as is the landscape it describes (Deleuze and Guattari, 1994: 169). And while such participation does not mean that all processes are the *result* of our attempts to comprehend them, there is – as the placebo effect illustrates, Greco points out – a 'sensitivity of the world to our interest in it' (Greco, 2005: 24).

That acknowledgement returns us to the various forms of 'cutting'[14] in which participants inevitably engage as they engage in framing practices.

Elsewhere I have argued for a notion of ethics as a form of enactment that attends to 'externalities'[15] not in order to include them but to consider their rearrangement into – or within – another frame (such as a piece of academic writing). Somewhat similarly, Mariam Fraser (2005) develops an argument for the notion of ethics as itself to be understood as an actualization within the various relations of prehensions.[16] Drawing on the work of Stengers and Whitehead, Fraser argues that ethics is about the rearrangement of these relations, about realizing the unrealized potential *through* participation. Rather than the production of judgements, it is the *shaping* of incidents and their participants that constitutes ethics: 'rather than judging ethics according to how well it is or is not able to judge a world that is external to it, its value lies in its own immanent actualization in a world in which it is, inextricably, implicated' (Fraser, 2005: 19). Of course it is important here is that one needs always to attend to the decisions that accompany framing practices. But crucially, nor is the case that just *any* ethics is possible. Whether one understands externalities as produced *from within* a frame, as 'exteriorized' as for Latour; or, as virtual, or as 'remainders' as Whitehead puts it, there is a sense in which these aspects 'belong' to the accomplished entity. Whitehead argued that by the very nature of producing a case, you have abstracted from the remainder of things such that novel relations 'tug' at that remainder (quoted in Fraser, 2005: 21). If these 'otherwise' elements are a resource for the future, it follows that beyond the acknowledgement of a necessary performativity to ethics, is the acknowledgement that something has been 'tethered'. The limitations are not material limitations on language, or reality's limitations on human imagination, but the present's on the future, that is, the (virtual) present on the paths of actualization. With this emphasis, Deleuze and Guattari's work becomes less fantastical than some have read it: it is precisely routed in the (potentialities of the) present. Likewise, Elizabeth Grosz's conclusions can be reread for the difference they contain: 'even with careful planning and preparation, the political alternatives to present domination are not there, simply waiting to be chosen, possible but not yet real. These alternatives, as Bergson recognized, are not alternatives, not possibilities, until they are brought into existence. The task is not so much to plan the future, to organize our resources to it, to envision it before it comes about, for this reduces the future to the present. It is to make the future, to invent it' (2004: 261). With these remarks, Grosz deflates the pomposity of much work which seems to believe one can move from the 'is' to the 'ought' without recognizing that the 'is' has already been subjected to all sorts of criteria of value in order to emerge and survive (that they have been given value, however, is not the same as saying they *should* be valued, as Fraser notes, 2006). Ethics becomes consonant with politics (as Latour also argues) because each can only be the practice of developing etho-ecological environments, arrangements and compositions. To invent these is not to be able to *direct* the entities sustained there, which only by their appearance suggest – and only *suggest* – the 'success' of any retrospectively imagined path of actualization. The impulse to offer optimism might lead one, with Grosz, to emphasize the productive role that any entity or composite has or *holds as potential* (and which only in that peculiar sense belongs to it), given the environment to sustain its emergence, given the right 'inventions'. But such optimism is to be tempered with all the hesitations that arise from acknowledgement that the reverberations of inventions may elaborate themselves in compositions and directions both unintended and unwelcome.

Afterword

At this historical juncture, when many might argue that sociocultural theory has taken a performative turn, in other intellectual arenas new theoretical interests and perspectives are already crowding its terrain, and complicating its certainties. It seems apposite, then, that this work should amount to a reflection on the promise of performativity as an ethical intervention. And indeed this book represents a journey, both that of a concept – performativity – and of my relation to the theoretical perspective within which it is ensconced (which is, but is also more than, a personal intellectual journey). I chose to emphasize a particular trajectory of this concept, from Nietzsche through Foucault to Judith Butler not least because I have sought to argue that the concept of performativity is indissociable from a critique of the 'value of values'. That is, the practice of giving-value has to be understood as a performative with the ability to create constituencies that are sustained and sustain in turn their effected element. I wanted to emphasize that to argue this is already a political intervention that attempts to interrupt any assumption of pure interiority. Another way of putting this might be to argue that whatever is regarded as existing by its own force alone or as an absolute – whether these be moral values, gender, absolute Alterity – is suspect, and ripe for critical reinscription in so far as one might regard it as composed within (or at the juncture of) the lines of the *dispositifs* by which it is sustained. Its emergence is relational, and the relations (of light, of speech, of power) that sustain it are contingent if not necessarily as fragile as the optimist implies. It is difficult work to imagine everything as composition, set in relation, to imagine even oneself as constituted *over* the relation with the other. It puts one at risk of psychosis, as Butler suggests, as one enters proximity with Descartes 'mad man' who doubts his own body, believing it glass. But it is precisely this we must doubt. Problematic too are those things we comprehend all too quickly as relational; to have one's father's gestures is not considered peculiar enough. If we are to understand the relation as performative, are we denying the relations between bodies that live, give birth, that die? If we think only of the positive dimensions of a 'spiritual' communion, do we continue the Pauline tradition unthinkingly? One has thus to recognize the specificities of the performance, its continuities not as natural certainly, nor as completely arbitrary, but as *trained* in the senses discussed here. And since one partakes in the world and is in that sense complicit at some level with the sustenance of all modes of understanding generation, this is an ethical issue. Moreover, because familial relations – especially the relation between parent and child – seem to confer a partiality that we sentimentalize and indulge all too readily,[1] it is incumbent upon one to interrogate the moments when Levinas's 'fact of chaining' confers value where it need not. There are and no doubt will be those who give performative repetitions *value* in abhorrent ways – I am thinking here of racism and instances of ethnic conflict – so that there is a need to question not necessarily the inevitability of repetition, but the *how* of that repetition. That is, by inserting and insisting on the contingencies of conjuring with ancestry, and by questioning the acceptance and comprehensibility of partiality with regard to the future. By pointing to perhaps the ethical question par excellence, the faces of others and others' children, whose world is also at stake, made possible or impossible by how one partakes in the present. At least, for this is not even to begin to mention the non-human, the things and habitats that such partiality also puts at risk. If this is a little smug, and verges on the moralism I suggested performativity had 'promised' not to become, one must also remember that one's own attentions are framed, and that there is violence in that framing. In attempting to respond, then, one is inevitably also entangled in decisions that ignore or cut away from things that are related and are therefore relevant. 'The ethical' is also a negotiation, then, with the non-ethical, a negotiation from which one never satisfactorily emerges.

To point to the conditions and complicities of one's own arguments and interventions confers a humility not because such a disposition is efficacious but because it is necessary. It is to reflect on the constraints and contingencies on our ways of thinking, and not least, as I have suggested here, of our ways of fearing. What one tries to avoid, as much as what one tries to bring about, informs political actions. These fears are not without reason, but they are sustained in one way or another so that become conditions and reference points thereafter. And because politics mobilizes itself around these as much as around utopian visions of futures or political processes, these should not be allowed to take on the status of innocent facts. Whether they enter into relations, or emerge within arguments, they are not remembered but deployed in order to make other connections possible.

We can 'reveal', 'expose' and understand these connections as political interventions. But perhaps the mode of ethical and political argumentation adopted alongside the concept of 'performativity' has moved too swiftly to confer on genealogical investigations this ability to investigate and *thereby* to refold, to rearrange, to even incite other possibilities (in)to the present. Deleuze's somewhat dangerous reading of Foucault's *dispositif* made clear that an apparatus is not there to be described, since the element it allows to emerge and which it sustains does not bear the traces of its own emergence. Indeed, if 'lines of light' are more than metaphorical in the imagined diagram of each *dispositif*, they preclude the desire that the other, neglected, incalculable, unaccounted or unchosen can be summoned to give witness. In debating how that which has value was *given* value genealogy cannot be figured as simply a realist enterprise except in so far as its reality might expand to include a kind of virtual reality. This would mean that what it can be said to provoke or prompt is qualified. That is, to imagine that aspects of a *dispositif* might behave in potentially new ways, the term 'potential' is to be understood as something that 'belongs' to that aspect in question (although belonging here is crucially understood as arranged across an emergent existence and its environment, as well as between a candidate to existence and its jury). Any attempt to direct the trembling that genealogical investigations may set in motion is for this reason alone going to be an arduous, even impossible, task. Thus the concern with the potentiality of 'the object' opens onto other concerns, ones that take us into a different litera-ture in so far as the potentiality that belongs to the object itself (including its maintenance of its own non-possibility) might return one to the 'interiority' which the mantra of coextensivity associated with performativity had seemingly dispersed. While this interiority – at least as potentiality – is not 'in' the object, it is also the case that it constitutes a challenge to performativity in so far as there is something – some capacity (to differentiate), some substance or some life – that cannot be rendered as part of the environment or *dispositif* and made, by fiat, coextensive once more. Creativity, self-organization and vitalism should not be understood simply to supersede performativity, even if – within the con-fines or 'environment' of feminism, say – these terms have appeared *as if* cri-tiques of this concept. That is to say that these critiques should not be understood as directed at a theoretical approach as such, to be used for point-scoring within an internal conversation that enables the 'performativity para-digm' to be toppled. Certainly there can be no question of brute, mute Reality that halts the conversations of theoretical work (Stengers 2002: 238), since the 'facts' are always ones that emerge and that are given value within particular assemblages. 'Nature' is produced and cannot be wheeled in to oppose, for instance, language. Rather, I have argued here that this 'vitalist' work might prompt reconsideration of one's participation within a wider composition or ecology. One cannot opt out of the assemblages within which one operates, for one is tied in a myriad of ways to their processes of creation. To create relevant knowledge, then, is to attach oneself in some way – since 'no knowledge is both relevant and detached' (Stengers, 2005: 1002) – and so to compose, even an academic text, is to enter into an assemblage both ethical and political. The challenge of complexity is not that of a different normative view of how the world works, but a challenge to assumptions that paths (of actualization) can always be known, that such prediction should be the aim. As I have argued, there is much in this work that challenges what 'performativity' has meant in feminist scholarship and beyond, which should not be minimized; but in this sense it adds meaning to Nietzsche's remark that when it comes to knowledge, we are strangers to ourselves. More than this, it suggests that we are engaged in modes of being that are in turn also modes of constituting the habitats in which other entities (concepts, organisms, objects) survive or disappear. To partake in these environments or assemblages, then, is to partake in the actualization of the present's potential, the composition of tomorrow.

Notes

INTRODUCTION

1. *11'09''01 – September 11*: A film by eleven directors; based on an idea by Alain Brigand; directed by Samira Makhmalbaf, Claude Lelouch, Youssef Chahine, Danis Tanovic, Idrissa Ouedraogo, Ken Loach, Alejandro Inarritu, Amos Gitai, Mira Nair, Sean Penn and Shohei Imamura. Galatée Films-Studio Canal, 2002.
2. As the philosophies of Sartre, as well as Adorno and Horkheimer explored.
3. I'm remembering Arendt's (1984) essay that defends thinking as an activity.
4. The images of Israeli soldiers removing settlers from the Gaza strip in 2005 prompted just such debates (see Shabi, 2006).
5. The word is Badiou's, which he takes from Leibniz (see Badiou 2003: 91).
6. This was the argument of my *Feminist Imagination: Genealogies in Feminist Thinking* (Sage, 1999).
7. As an epigraph to Chapter 1 of 'Coldness and Cruelty' in *Masochism* (1989).
8. If it is even that. I'm drawing, light-heartedly here, on Arendt, 1959b. For more serious engagement with Arendt on issues of religion and 'secularism' see Bell, 2005.

CHAPTER 1 THE PROMISE OF PERFORMATIVITY: THEORY AND/AS POLITICAL ETHIC

1. Moreover, in so far as the term culture still subtends an obligation to revisit the nature v. cultural debate, it tarries with an argument that this work would interrogate (as Derrida so masterfully did, see Derrida, 1977/1967). Further, it requires a rupturing from the sociological tendency to surrender the study of process of cultural reproduction to a form of historicism in which explanation for the current state of affairs is dolefully sought in the specific historical contingencies of the present as if they had just arrived here, with no ongoing rumbling directions to speak of.
2. As presented so graphically in the film *Boys Don't Cry* in which the true

story of Brandon illustrates the dangers of moving outside heteronorma-
tivity: when the bureaucratic police database 'reveals' that Brandon is
listed there as female, eclipsing and trumping his self-identification and
presentation, the reaction of the men in the group of friends into which he
had settled was one of violence (dir. Kimberley Peirce, 1999 Killer/Hart-
Sharp). Butler argues furthermore, that the film raises the difficulties of
speaking about bodies and pleasures. It raises the question of the complex
relation of gender identity to anatomy, since one couldn't say that
Brandon denies his anatomy exactly, but erotically 'deploys' that anatomy
'for the purposes of a reciprocal erotic fantasy' (2004a: 143). It is certainly
not enough to say that Brandon does himself as a boy in order to pursue
lesbianism, since this is to tidy a more complicated scenario in which
gender itself has its pleasures for Brandon, as well as to avoid seeing that
'no anatomy enters gender without being "done" in some way' (2004a:
143).

3. One could say they only become possibilities after their enactment or
actualization (see Chapter 6).

4. As Butler points out in her riposte to those who would regard matters of
sexuality as 'merely cultural' (Butler, 1997c), there are other genealogies
one might choose to evoke. Althusser's insistence that 'an ideology always
exists in an apparatus, and in its practice or practices ... its existence is
always material' furnishes her with a precedent in her claim that ideolog-
ical, 'cultural' issues are inseparable from the apparatus of power that
preside over forms of production. Any dismissal of queer politics as identitarian and concerned only with matters of social recognition fails to
remember the fundamentals of neo-Marxism. She recalls that just as for
Marx 'the economic' is an abstraction, so too is compulsory heterosexuality as socialist feminists have long argued. They are abstractions, further,
that come to delimit both the modes of production and the modes of
social association permitted, constraining the subject within their arrangements, requiring that s/he approximate the normative or become abject.
Butler writes: 'To insist that the social forms of sexuality not only exceed
but confound heterosexual kinship arrangements as well as reproduction
is also to argue that what qualifies as a person and as a sex will be radically altered – an argument that is not merely cultural, but which confirms the place of sexual regulation as a mode of producing the subject'
(1997c: 276).

5. I explored this relation between Descartes and the experience of not
owning one's body in relation to transsexualism in 'Sounding the Siren'
(1994).

6. Indeed, another manifestation of this same logic in Butler's work is her
argument that because one's body is never only one's own, and because

we struggle for bodies which aren't only ours, 'the body has its invariably public dimension' (2004b: 26). To act in relation to one's embodiment, in the name of that which most immediately belongs to oneself – my body, its integrity, 'these hands' – paradoxically make one a public actor. It has been given and is sustained by others. Actions in its name will cast a net that will potentially entangle many more than 'oneself'.

7. In the 1975–9 period in Cambodia Pol Pot established Democratic Kampuchea and an estimated 1.7 million perished from execution, torture, starvation or untreated illness. See e.g. Kiernan (2002). On the difficult pursuit of justice see Fawthorp and Jarvis (2004).

8. The defiance of traditional dance also arises in Chanrithy Him (2000) where she tells of the exhilaration of taking part in traditional folk dances inside 'refugee' camps in Cambodia from where she and her siblings later escaped to Canada. See her moving biography *When Broken Glass Floats: Growing Up under the Khmer Rouge* (2000).

9. Hamera understands this through Bakhtin's notion of 'answerability'. She writes that 'answerability is ambivalent – at its most generative it seems to deploy art to answer back; but at its most impotent, constrains the individual to the reaction of singular subjects condemned to answer to, or "rent" meaning' (2005: 99).

10. Patraka (1999) argues that representations of the Holocaust – for example, in theatre – 'mark and celebrate the goneness of what we want never to exist again – Nazism and the Holocaust – even as we want to create relationships to other events and cultural conditions in the past and to a present in which genocide has not disappeared' (1999: 5). Such representations inevitably foreground their constructed nature since they are the staging of where one was not, seeking to represent what cannot be re-enacted. But they are also accountable in the sense that the events which the term names were once enacted such that there is 'a pressure of the thing done on the doing': 'in the Holocaust performative, play [or destabilization, subversion or transgression] is limited by accountability' (1999: 7).

11. Hamera notes Ben's disappointment that his daughters are not interested in learning the traditional dance and so do not continue the tradition.

12. Afary and Anderson have suggested that Foucault was seduced by a drama he understood as between Khomeini and the very scene of politics. In the Revolution he saw a 'political spirituality', a collective will, that 'abstraction in political philosophy ... in the flesh' (Foucault, in Afary and Anderson, 2005: 221).

13. This focus on the attention to the term 'spirituality' lends some support to Afary and Anderson's controversial suggestion that Foucault's last works should be understood as a response to the negative reactions to his

articles on Iran. I would not, however, wish to sign up to the wider claims made in that book.

14. Afary and Anderson also suggest that the later volumes be understood as not only a reaching back into the history of the Western attitudes to sexuality, but also, framed through Foucault's 'orientalism', as an attempt to understand the practices of modern Middle East and North Africa.

15. Christianity disturbed this care of the self by placing an emphasis on salvation. It introduced the notion that one could be saved by God for one's exemplary life (Foucault, 1997/1984).

CHAPTER 2 GENEALOGY, GENERATION AND PARTIALITY

1. This is a tendency they find exemplified in Jean-Luc Nancy's (1991) *The Inoperative Community* for example.

2. As Critchley describes Levinas's argument, in *Ethics, Politics, Subjectivity*, 1999: 183.

3. In the manner that Judith Butler describes in *The Psychic Life of Power*.

4. As I argued in *Performativity and Belonging* (1999b).

5. In *Totality and Infinity* (1969) Levinas argues that in erotic love the lovers maintain their duality. Erotic desire always stumbles on the duality of the lovers' existence – the 'pathos of love' as Levinas refers to it in *Time and the Other* – and the I falls back upon itself, retains its separateness. Absolute fusion is impossible: existence can be communicated but not shared. But love is not friendship, and the relationship is not social. Levinas uses the term 'voluptuosity' to try to express what he means by the non-sociality of two lovers. There is not a third party in intimacy that would make the relationship social, but voluptuosity is the affirmation of the other as sentient. More than this, the sentiment is shared; is identical – love is a 'spontaneous consciousness' (1969: 265). The freedom of the other is, and has to be, untamed for voluptuosity to remain; power and possession are remote here. The lover thus retains his/her alterity, and has to do so for erotic desire to remain as such; in the identification the alterity of the Beloved is maintained, and this duality fuels voluptuosity (1969: 270). Love is not love of the Other exactly, but is a searching relationship to the infinitely future, a 'delight in the unparalleled conjuncture of identification' (1969: 266). 'Voluptuosity aims not at the Other but at his voluptuosity; it is voluptuosity of voluptuosity, love of the love of the other' (1969: 266).

6. 'Reflections on Little Rock' (1959a). See Bell, *Feminist Imagination* (1999) for fuller discussion.

7. According to her biographer, Elisabeth Young-Bruehl, Arendt felt that the parents of the children entering the hostile environment were forcing the child to treat education as a means for social advancement, denying the child the 'absolute protection of dignity' that her own mother had given her, instructing her to leave social situations where she was unwanted (1982: 311). Arendt wrote to Ellison, agreeing that she had not understood this ideal of sacrifice, that she had been unappreciative of the 'element of elementary, bodily fear in the situation' as an initiation into the realities of a racist society (in Young-Bruehl, 1982: 316).

8. A position that can also be voiced in more violent ways that oppose the embrace of multiculturalism, see Euben's discussion of *jihad* and martyrdom in 'Killing for Politics' (2002).

CHAPTER 3 NEGOTIATING THE NON-ETHICAL: ON 'ETHICAL FEMINISM'

1. Although Gilligan has emphasized that the notion of a different voice should be understood as characterized by the mode of reasoning and not by the gender of the speaker, it is associated by her and by others, with women, whose socially defined roles overdetermine them as those who will value the connections between people over 'the (moral) law'. Unsurprisingly therefore, Gilligan's work has been heavily criticized, not least for its tendencies toward essentialist modes of thought (as if being female was all that was needed to produce caring behaviour), as well as for its naivety in thinking these themes are spontaneously produced (were the responses an effect of the interviewees in Gilligan's study responding as women 'should'). It has also been seen as dangerously close to a sort of 'slave morality' where care is extended to all, including one's abuser (Card, 1990) and as unable to satisfactorily distinguish between appropriate and inappropriate forms of 'care' (Jaggar, 1995).

  Nevertheless, the notion of care has been enormously influential, connecting with developments elsewhere within feminist thought and with a wider mainstream search within ethics for an alternative to the impartial and universalist ethical subject of the Kantian and utilitarian frameworks which had dominated ethical philosophy (and as evidenced in the revival of interest in Aristotelian ethics with its emphasis on virtue and community) (Friedman, 2000: 207). Many feminists were intrigued to explore the potential to be wrought by placing care and connection at the centre of their analyses. The term provides an umbrella term for wide-ranging considerations of women's everyday interactions as gendered ethical practices, from styles of conversation, to mothering practices, to embodied negotiations of space. Moreover, placing 'care' centrally, several feminists have suggested, would provide for an improved focus for feminist political demands, and if these demands are met, an improved world where care and connection counter the tendencies of the masculinist world to individualist approaches to life (this has taken many forms, e.g. Jaggar, 1995; Noddings, 1984; Ruddick, 1989; for a more recent example in context of women in British politics, see MacKay, 2001).

2. That is, feminist ethics could be said, by the end of the 1980s, to have been committed to two principles: first, an engagement with ethics as *embodied and situated* that arose as a counter to the history of thinking the ethical subject as an abstract rational code-following ideal being; and secondly, an engagement with an appreciation of *difference*, that arose out of the concern that abstraction had effectively eliminated the central point of ethics, that is, to be responsiveness to the (concrete) other (Benhabib, 1987: 89). These principles, which continue to inform feminist work (see Walker, 1998), engage with intersubjectivity as an embodied, visceral encounter at which differences are not only negotiated but, simultaneously, constituted.

3. See Brown, 1995 for discussion of this term; also see Butler and Cornell in conversation with Cheah and Grosz (Butler and Cornell, 1998), for use of the term 'wounded', and Denise Riley's *Words of Selves* (2000).

4. The phrase is Nietzsche's, or Zarathustra's, who describes his state thus, but who is also able despite this anger to see into the future, to create a future and a bridge to the future (1954: 250–1). Unlike 'us', who are the fools who fall into our melancholy and dwell in it.

5. In a different way, through a discussion of Simone de Beauvoir and Richard Wright, Chapter 3 of my book *Feminist Imagination* (1999a) also answers this debate about *ressentiment*.

6. And this was an aspect of Levinas's thought that has given rise to much debate, given Judaism's tension between the particularity of response to Jewish peoples and the purported universalism of Levinas's thought.

7. 'The humanity of consciousness is definitely not in its powers, but in its responsibility: in passivity, in reception, in obligation with regard to the other. It is the other who is first, and there the question of my sovereign consciousness is no longer the first question. I advocate, as in the title of one of my books, the humanism of the other man' (Levinas 1998b: 104).

8. This is, as I understand it, close to Connolly's argument (1998, 1999).

9. Which is on reflection rather close to Caputo's argument that we have reached the end of ethics: 'This discourse proceeds on the belief that ethics ends where singularity begins, which means where existence begins, since singulars are the sole existents. When the seas of singularity get rough, when the winds of existence blow up, ethics generally goes below'

(2000: 190). The difference is that Caputo sees ethics as existing in times of difficulty, whereas in my formulation, the term ethics is retained to described the processes of checking that accompany political performatives.

CHAPTER 4 RHETORICAL FIGURES: ON 'DANGEROUS THOUGHT', FEAR AND POLITICS

1. To recall one of Derrida's trains of thought in *Spectres of Marx* (1994).
2. Indeed, Nussbaum's review essay is itself highly rhetorical; in one paragraph she repeats 'before Butler' six times in order to reinforce her point that many of Butler's arguments are 'not especially new'.

CHAPTER 5 NAUSEA'S POTENTIAL? GENEALOGY AND POLITICS

1. A contrast is emerging here with the work of Ranciere. See Michael Shapiro, 2004.
2. Callon is distancing himself from the influential older work of Coarse (1960), who argued that agents should be understood as having the capacity to sort out their externalities without intervention by public authorities except when property rights are not clearly defined. Where they are not public institutions are required to facilitate the negotiations.
3. Latour has reflected: 'At the time the word network, like Deleuze and Guattari's term rhizome, clearly meant a series of transformations – translations, transductions – which could not be captured by using the traditional terms of social theory. With the new popularisation of the word network it now means transport without deformation, an instantaneous unmediated access to every piece of information. That is exactly the opposite of what we meant' (1999: 15).
4. It lends itself, furthermore, to the notion that the task is itself a moral one, a part of Latour's moralist chorus, dangerously close to the kind of moralism that we had thought a Foucauldian-influenced concept of performativity promised against (Chapter 1).
5. Although it perhaps suggests – as indeed Fraser (2006), drawing on the arguments of Whitehead, argues – that what is sustained has attained *value* in some way (2006: 65–6). That it has attained value is not to say that these values are necessarily to *be* valued (2006: 65).

CHAPTER 6 PERFORMATIVITY CHALLENGED? CREATIVITY AND THE RETURN OF INTERIORITY

1. Where 'investiture' here refers to the sense in which bodies are invested with and by power/knowledge relations.
2. Prigogine asserts that the results of non-equilibrium thermodynamics are close to the views expressed by Bergson and Whitehead. 'Nature is indeed related to the creation of unpredictable novelty, where the possible is richer than the real. Our universe has followed a path involving a succession of bifurcations. While other universes may have followed other paths, we are fortunate that ours has led to life, culture and the arts' (1997: 72).
3. For a clear explanation of why assemblages are extensions, see Colebrook (2002) from whom I have borrowed this example.
4. Desire is an expression of Deleuzean difference, since desire is precisely the impetus for becoming other (differing); desire doesn't arrive from a lack that desire then seeks to fulfil but is more akin to a Nietzschean will to power, the pure affirmation of difference for its own sake.
5. Such as Ansell Pearson reads in Nietzsche's work (1997) and Beatrice Han discusses in somewhat different terms in relation to Foucault (2002).
6. Interestingly, the concept of vitalism has itself been recast. 'Preformism' was exactly the charge against classic vitalism, which its critics understood as teleological – exemplified most clearly in embryology. Now the tables are turned! Bergson–Deleuze have 'rescued' vitalism from preformism of which others – Judith Butler for example – are accused. Thanks to my colleague Monica Greco for this astute observation.
7. This internal cause is the efficient cause that plays the central role in Scholastic ontological foundations (Hardt, 1993: 5).
8. At this juncture one begins to see the link with creative evolution which feminist theorist Elizabeth Grosz has recently explored, the powerful reassertion of duration and the vital process of creativity with its profound implications for the centrality of sexual difference. But to remain with the principle task here, what requires explanation is how this Bergsonian inspiration in Deleuze collides with versions of performativity that currently circulate.
9. As Hardt suggests, this is therefore an affirmation of the efficient cause (virtual-actual) over the formal cause (possible-real).
10. Although arguably it returns to an older understanding of mimesis such as that articulated by Adorno and Horkheimer (see also Bell, 1999a, where I discuss Butler's mimesis in relation to Adorno and Horkheimer).
11. In this way Deleuze and Guattari discuss 'minor literatures'. Bogue explains how the Prague dialect, influenced by Czech, was an impoverished German. It was a language which had been 'deterritorialized' in that

Prague German was detached from its native context, rendered artificial through its heavy bureaucratic associations and at the same time destabilized by the way it was used (ungrammatical constructions, words with multiple and shifting non-standard meanings, accents and gestures, etc.). By Prague Jews it was on the one hand embraced and elaborated, enriched, or else it was impoverished further as in Kafka who limited its vocabulary, avoided metaphor etc. thereby imbuing it with an 'affective intensity' (Bogue, 2003: 117). Kafka exaggerated tendencies in the minor use of German by Prague Jews. Exaggerating these tendencies is one way that the assemblage is made to 'quiver'.

12. As discussed in my paper 'The Burden of Sensation and the Ethics of Form: Watching "Capturing the Friedmans"', presented at Goldsmiths College, February 2006. Here I argue that the watching and 'evaluation' of a documentary film is already within the cinema-assemblage, not only because one has paid a price for the ticket, but because one's evaluation of the truth of a documentary cannot relate to anything but the sensations of cinematic experience.

13. Fraser is drawing on Whitehead here, who argued that the pattern is itself shaped by how it is perceived/prehended. 'Every prehension consists of three factors: a) the "subject" which is prehending, namely, the actual entity in which that prehension is a concrete element; (b) the "datum" which is prehended; (c) the "subjective form" which is *how* that subject prehends that datum' (Whitehead, 1978/1929: 23).

14. I'm referring back to Barthes (1975) here, but also to the work of Marilyn Strathern (1996; 2002), which I have used in other work (see e.g. Bell, 2001b).

15. See Callon, 1998; Strathern, 2002 on externalities. My paper is entitled 'Enacting Ethics: Reading the Laming Report' (2006) Paper presented at the Institute for the Sociology of Law, Onati, Spain 2005 and the International Sociological Association Conference, Durban, South Africa, July 2006. It is partly due to the difficulties of arguing for interiorities as folds, and thereby suggesting that cuts are not gaps but the redistribution of the continuity, that Badiou criticizes Deleuze (on Liebniz) and distances his own perspective (1994: 59). In Badiou truth punctures, whereas in Deleuze as we have seen, entities emerge without interruption. The only 'cut' allowed in Deleuze, according to Badiou, is actually an inflection (1994: 59–60). Because I am using the notion of a cut here to point to the forms of framing that occur as techniques articulate and construct problems, issues or entities, this would appear to confuse languages. However, the emergent entity is not understood here as a cut or interruption in Badiou's sense, and it is precisely because it cannot truly exclude the externalities that 'belong' to it that

this perspective differs from Badiou's emphasis on the event.

16. Fraser does so not in the abstract terms in which I am presenting her, but through an analysis of the so-called 'Wesbecker' trial. *Joyce Fentress et al vs. Eli Lilly* (1994), the first case against Prozac to reach a jury, was closely tied to the question of the integrity of Lilly's methods for testing Prozac in the clinic.

AFTERWORD

1. I am thinking here of the work of Lauren Berlant (1997); but also, although I have discovered it too late to discuss in detail here, the work of Lee Edelman, whose argument in *No Future* to 'resist the appeal of futurity' (2004: 17) especially in so far as the figure of the child is the pre-eminent figure through which such an appeal is made, would contrast with the one suggested here, although the intentions in so doing are more resonant with the arguments of that chapter.

References

Adorno, Theodor and Horkheimer, Max (1986/1944) *Dialectics of Enlightenment*, Verso: London.

Afary, Janet and Anderson, Kevin (2005) *Foucault and the Iranian Revolution: Gender and the Seductions of Islamism*, Chicago: Chicago University Press.

Agamben, Giorgio (1999) *Potentialities: Collected Essays in Philosophy* (trans. Daniel Heller-Roasen), Stanford: Stanford University Press.

Ahmed, Sara (1998) *Differences That Matter: Feminist Theory and Postmodernism*, Cambridge: Cambridge University Press.

—— (2000) *Strange Encounters: Embodied Others in Postcoloniality*, Routledge: New York.

Ansell Pearson, Keith (1997) *Viroid Life*, London: Routledge

—— (1999) 'Bergson and Creative Evolution/Involution: Exposing the Transcendental Illusion of Organismic Life' in Mullarkey, J. (ed.), *The New Bergson*, Manchester: Manchester University Press.

Arendt, Hannah (1959a) 'Reflections on Little Rock', *Dissent* 6(1): 45–56.

—— (1959b) *The Human Condition*, New York: Doubleday and Co.

—— (1963) *Between Past and Future: Six Exercises in Political Thought*, New York: Meridian.

—— (1984) 'Thinking and Moral Considerations', *Social Research* 51(1): 7–37.

Austin, J. L. (2004/1962) 'How to Do Things With Words', in J. Rivkin and M. Ryan (eds), *Literary Theory: An Anthology*, Oxford: Blackwell.

Badiou, Alain (1994) 'Gilles Deleuze, The Fold: Leibniz and the Baroque', in C. V. Boundas and D. Olkowski (eds), *Gilles Deleuze and the Theater of Philosophy*, New York and London: Routledge.

—— (2000) *Ethics: An Essay on the Understanding of Evil* (trans. P. Hallward), London: Verso.

—— (2003) *Infinite Thought: Truth and the Return to Philosophy* (trans. Oliver Feltham and Justin Clemens), London: Continuum.

Barad, Karen (2003) 'Posthumanist Performativity: Toward an Understanding of How Matter Comes to Matter', *Signs* 28(3): 801–31.

Bar On, Bat-Ami (1998) 'Everyday Violence and Ethico-Political Crisis' in Bat-Ami Bar On and Ann Ferguson (eds), *Daring to Be Good: Essays in Feminist Ethico-Politics*, New York: Routledge.

Barry, Andrew (2001) *Political Machines: Governing a Technological Society*, London: Continuum.

Barthes, R. (1975) *The Pleasure of the Text* (trans. Richard Miller), New York: Hill and Wang.

Bell, Vikki (1994) 'Sounding the Siren: Ambiguity and the Gender *Dispositif*', *Modern and Renaissance Studies*, Nottingham: Nottingham University.

—— (1999a) *Feminist Imagination: Genealogies in Feminist Theory*, London: Sage.

—— (ed.) (1999b) *Performativity and Belonging*, London: Sage.

—— (2001a) 'Negotiating and Narrating Emplacement: Belonging and Conflict in Northern Ireland', *New Formations* Spring No. 41: 61–86.

—— (2001b) 'The Phone, the Father and Other Becomings: On Households (and Theories) that no longer Hold', *Cultural Values* 5(3): 383–402.

—— (2005) 'On Secular Ethics: An Essay with Flannery O'Connor and Hannah Arendt', *Theory, Culture & Society* 22(2): 1–27.

Benhabib, Seyla (1987) 'The Generalised and the Concrete Other: The Kohlberg-Gilligan Controversy and Feminist Theory', in S. Benhabib and D. Cornell (eds), *Feminism as Critique*, Cambridge: Polity.

Bergson, Henri (1911) *Creative Evolution* (trans. A. Mitchell), London: MacMillan.

Berlant, Lauren (1997) *The Queen of America Goes to Washington City*, Durham, NC: Duke University Press.

Berube, Michael (2000) 'The Return of Realism and the Future of Contingency', in J. Butler, J. Guillory and K. Thomas (eds), *What's Left of Theory? New Work on the Politics of Literary Theory*, New York: Routledge

Bogue, Ronald (2003) 'Minority, Territory, Music', in Jean Khalfa (ed.), *An Introduction to the Philosophy of Gilles Deleuze*, London: Continuum.

Boyarin, Daniel (1997) *Unheroic Conduct: The Rise of Heterosexuality and the Invention of the Jewish Man*, Berkeley and Los Angeles: University of California Press.

—— and Boyarin, Jonathan (1993) 'Diaspora: Generation and the Ground of Jewish Identity', *Critical Inquiry* 19: 693–725.

Boyarin, Jonathan and Boyarin, Daniel (1995) 'Self-Exposure as Theory: The Double Mark of the Male Jew', in D. Battaglia (ed.), *Rhetorics of Self-Making*, Berkeley and Los Angeles: University of California Press.

Braidotti, Rosi (2002) *Metamorphoses: Towards a Materialist Theory of Becoming*, Cambridge: Polity.

Brown, Wendy (1995) *States of Injury: Power and Freedom in Late Modernity*, Princeton, NJ: Princeton University Press.

—— (2001) *Politics Out of History* Princeton: Princeton University Press.

Buck-Morss, Susan (2000) *Dreamworlds: The Passing of Mass Utopia in East and West*, Cambridge, MA: MIT Press.

Butler, Judith (1990) *Gender Trouble*, New York: Routledge.

—— (1993) *Bodies That Matter*, London: Routledge.

—— (1997a) *Excitable Speech*, Routledge: New York.

—— (1997b) *The Psychic Life of Power: Theories in Subjection*, Stanford, CA: Stanford University Press.

—— (1997c) 'Merely Cultural', *Social Text 52/53* 15(3&4): 264–77.

—— (2004a) *Undoing Gender*, New York: Routledge.

—— (2004b) *Precarious Life*, London: Verso.

—— and Cornell, Drucilla (1998) 'The Future of Sexual Difference: An Interview with Judith Butler and Drucilla Cornell', *Diacritics* 28(1): 19–42.

Callon, Michel (1998) 'An Essay on Framing and Overflowing: Economic Externalities Revisited by Sociology', in Michel Callon (ed.), *The Laws of the Markets*, Oxford: Blackwell.

Caputo, John D. (2000) *More Radical Hermeneutics: On Not Knowing Who We Are*, Bloomington, IN: Indiana University Press

Card, Claudia (1990) 'Gender and Moral Luck', in Owen Flanagan and Amelie Rorty (eds), *Identity, Character and Morality*, Cambridge, MA: MIT Press.

Chanter, Tina (1995) *Ethics of Eros: Irigaray's Rewriting of the Philosophers*, Routledge: London.

Cheah, Pheng (1996) 'Mattering', *Diacritics* 26(1): 108–39.

Cilliers, Paul (2005) 'Complexity, Deconstruction and Relativism', *Theory, Culture & Society* 22(5): 255–67.

Coarse, E. R. (1960) 'The Problem of Social Costs', *Journal of Law and Economics* 3: 1–44.

Cockburn, Cynthia (1998) *The Space between Us: Negotiating Gender and National Identities in Conflict*, London: Zed Books.

Colebrook, Claire (2002) *Gilles Deleuze*, London: Routledge.

Connolly, William (1998) 'The Ethical Sensibility of Michel Foucault', in J. Moss (ed.), *The Later Foucault*, London: Sage

—— (1999) 'Suffering, Justice, and the Politics of Becoming', in D. Campbell and M. Shapiro (eds), *Moral Spaces: Rethinking Ethics and World Politics*, Minneapolis: University of Minnesota Press.

Cornell, Drucilla (1995) 'What is an Ethical Feminism?', in Seyla Benhabib, Judith Butler, Drucilla Cornell and Nancy Fraser (eds), *Feminist Contentions: A Philosophical Exchange*, New York: Routledge

Critchley, Simon (1999) *Ethics, Politics, Subjectivity*, Verso: London.

Davies, P. and Gribbin, J. (1991) *The Matter Myth: Beyond Chaos and Complexity*, London: Penguin.

Davis, Scott Grady (1992) *Warcraft and the Fragility of Virtue: An Essay in Aristotelian Ethics*, Moscow, ID: University of Idaho Press.

De Boer, T. (1986) 'An Ethical Transcendental Philosophy', in R. Cohen (ed.), *Face to Face with Levinas*, New York: SUNY Press.

DeLanda, Manuel (2002) *Intensive Science and Virtual Philosophy*, London: Continuum.

Deleuze, Gilles (1988/1966) *Bergsonism* (trans. Hugh Tomlinson and Barbara Habberjam), New York: Zone Books.

Deleuze, Gilles (1988/1986) *Foucault* (trans. S. Hand), London: Athlone.

—— (1989) 'Coldness and Cruelty', in Gilles Deleuze and Leopold von Sacher-Masoch, *Masochism*, New York: Zone Books.

—— (1992) 'What is a Dispositif?', in Armstrong, Timothy, *Michel Foucault: Philosopher* (trans. Timothy Armstrong), Hemel Hempstead: Harvester Wheatsheaf.

—— (1995) *Negotiations 1972–1990* (trans. Martin Joughin), New York: Columbia University Press.

—— (1999/1956) 'Bergson's Conception of Difference', in J. Mullarkey (ed.), *The New Bergson*, Manchester: Manchester University Press.

—— (2004/1994) *Difference and Repetition* (trans. Paul Patton), London: Continuum.

—— and Guattari, Felix (1984) *Anti-Oedipus: Capitalism and Schizophrenia*, London: Athlone Press.

—— and Guattari, Felix (1988) *A Thousand Plateaus: Capitalism and Schizophrenia*, London: Athlone Press.

—— and Guattari, Felix (1994) *What is Philosophy?* (trans. Graham Burchell), Verso: London.

—— and Parnet, Claire (2002/1997) *Dialogues II*, London: Continuum

Derrida, Jacques (1977/1967) *Of Grammatology* (trans. Gayatri Spivak), Baltimore, MD: John Hopkins University Press.

—— (1978) 'Violence and Metaphysics', in *Writing and Difference* (trans. Alan Bass), Chicago: University of Chicago Press.

—— (1982) *Margins of Philosophy* (trans. Alan Bass), Chicago: Chicago University Press.

—— (1990) 'Force of law: "The Mystical Foundation of Authority"', *Cardozo Law Review: Deconstruction and the Possibility of Justice* 11(5–6): 920–1045.

—— (1994) *Spectres of Marx*, New York: Routledge.

—— (1995) *The Gift of Death* (trans. David Wills), Chicago: University of Chicago Press

Descartes, René (1992/1641) *A Discourse on Method: Meditations and Principles*, London: Everyman.

De Vries, Hent (1997) 'Violence and Testimony', in H. De Vries and S. Weber (eds), *Violence, Identity and Self-determination*, Stanford: Stanford University Press.

Diamond, Elin (1997) *Unmaking Mimesis*, London: Routledge.

Edelman, Lee (2004) *No Future: Queer Theory and the Death Drive*, Durham, NC: Duke University Press.

Euben, Roxanna (2002) 'Killing (For) Politics: *Jihad*, Martyrdom and Political Action', *Political Theory* 30(1): 4–35.

Fawthorp, T. and Jarvis, H. (2004) *Getting Away with Genocide? Elusive Justice and the Khmer Rouge Tribunal*, London: Pluto

Flax, J. (1993) *Disputed Subjects: Essays on Psychoanalysis, Politics and Philosophy*, New York: Routledge.

Fleiger, Jerry A. (2000) 'Becoming-Woman: Deleuze, Schreber and Molecular Identification', in Ian Buchanan and Claire Colebrook (eds), *Deleuze and Feminist Theory*, Edinburgh: Edinburgh University Press.

Foucault, Michel (1975) *Discipline and Punish*, Harmondsworth: Penguin

—— (1981) *The History of Sexuality Volume One: An Introduction*, Penguin: Harmondsworth.

—— (1984) 'Preface', in G. Deleuze and F. Guattari, *Anti-Oedipus: Capitalism and Schizophrenia*, London: Athlone Press.

—— (1985) *The History of Sexuality Volume Two: The Use of Pleasure* (trans. Hurley, Robert), Harmondsworth: Penguin (first published in French 1984).

—— (1986) 'Nietzsche, Genealogy, History', in Paul Rabinow (ed.), *The Foucault Reader*, Harmondsworth: Penguin.

—— (1988) *The History of Sexuality Volume Three: The Care of the Self* (trans. Hurley, Robert), New York: Vintage Books (first published in French 1984).

—— (1996) 'The Masked Philosopher', in S. Lotringer (ed.), *Foucault Live*, New York: Semiotext(e).

—— (1997/1984) 'The Ethics of the Concern of the Self as a Practice of Freedom', in Paul Rabinow (ed.), *Michel Foucault: Ethics, Subjectivity and Truth* Essential Works of Michel Foucault Volume 1 (trans. Robert Hurley et al.) New York: The New Press.

Fraser, Mariam (2002) 'What is the Matter of Feminist Criticism?', *Economy & Society* 31(4): 606–25.

—— (2005) 'Moral Measures' (forthcoming).

—— (2006) 'The Ethics of Reality and Virtual Reality: Latour, Facts and Values', *The History of the Human Sciences* 19(2): 45–72.

Fraser, Nancy (1997) 'Heterosexism, Misrecognition and Capitalism: A Response to Butler', *Social Text 52/53* 15(3–4): 279–89.

Friedman, Marilyn (2000) 'Feminism in ethics: Conceptions of autonomy', in M. Fricker and J. Hornsby (eds), *The Cambridge Companion to Feminism in Philosophy*, Cambridge: Cambridge University Press.

Gilroy, Paul (1993) *The Black Atlantic: Modernity and Double Consciousness*, London: Verso.

—— (1997) 'Diaspora and the Detours of Identity', in K. Woodward (ed.), *Identity and Difference*, London: Sage/OUP.

—— (2000) *Between Camps: Nations, Cultures and the Allure of Race*, Penguin: London.

Gordon, Colin (ed.) (1980) *Michel Foucault: Selected Interviews and Writings 1972–1977* (trans. Colin Gordon), Brighton: Harvester Press.

Greco, Monica (2005) 'On the Vitality of Vitalism', *Theory, Culture & Society* 22(1): 15–28.

Grosz, Elizabeth (2004) *The Nick of Time: Politics, Evolution and the Untimely*, Durham, NC: Duke University Press.

—— (2005) *Time Travels: Feminism, Nature, Power*, Durham, NC: Duke University Press.

Gutting, Gary (2001) *French Philosophy in the Twentieth Century*, Cambridge: Cambridge University Press.

Hamera, Judith (2005) 'The Answerability of Memory: "Saving" Khmer Classical Dance', in Akbar Abbas and John Nguyet Erni (eds), *Internationalising Cultural Studies*, Oxford: Blackwell.

Han, Beatrice (2002/1998) *Foucault's Critical Project* (trans. Edward Pile), Stanford, CA: Stanford University Press.

Hand, Sean (ed.) (1989) *The Levinas Reader*, Oxford: Blackwell.

Haraway, Donna (1991) *Simians, Cyborgs and Women: The Reinvention of Nature*, London: Free Association Books.

Hardt, Michael (1993) *Gille Deleuze: An Apprenticeship in Philosophy*, London: UCL Press.

Hayles, Katherine (1990) *Chaos Bound: Orderly Disorder in Contemporary Literature and Science*, Ithaca, NY: Cornell University Press.

—— (1999) *How We Became Post-Human: Virtual Bodies in Cybernetics, Literature and Informatics*, Chicago: University of Chicago Press.

Hennessey, Rosemary (2000) *Profit and Pleasure: Sexual Identities in Late Capitalism*, New York: Routledge.

Him, Chanrithy (2000) *When Broken Glass Floats: Growing Up Under the Khmer Rouge*, New York: Norton.

Honig, Bonnie (1992) 'Arendt and the Politics of Identity', in J. Butler and J. Scott (eds), *Feminists Theorise the Political*, New York: Routledge.

Jaggar, Alison (1995) 'Caring as a Feminist Practice of Moral Reason', in Virginia Held (ed.), *Justice and Care: Essential Readings in Feminist Ethics*, Boulder, CO: Westview.

—— (2000) 'Feminist Ethics', in Hugh LaFollette (ed.), *The Blackwell Guide to Ethical Theory*, Oxford: Blackwell.

Jonas, Hans (2005) 'The Burden and Blessing of Mortality', in Mariam Fraser and Monica Greco (eds), *The Body: A Reader*, London: Routledge.

Keane, Helen and Rosengarten, Marsha (2002) 'On the Biology of Sexed Bodies', *Australian Feminist Studies* 17(39): 261–76.

Khalfa, Jean (ed.) (2003) *An Introduction to the Philosophy of Gilles Deleuze*, London: Continuum.

Kiernan, Ben (2002) *The Pol Pot Regime: Race, Power and Genocide in*

Cambodia under the Khmer Rouge, 1975–79 (2nd Edition), New Haven, CT: Yale University Press.

Kirby, Vicki (1997) *Telling Flesh: The Substance of the Corporeal*, New York: Routledge.

Kristeva, Julia (1986) 'Women's Time', in T. Moi (ed.), *The Kristeva Reader*, New York: Columbia University Press.

Latour, Bruno (1993) *We Have Never Been Modern* (trans. Catherine Porter), London: Harvester Wheatsheaf.

—— (1999) 'On recalling ANT', in J. Law and J. Hassard (eds), *Actor Network Theory and After*, Oxford: Blackwell.

—— (2004) *Politics of Nature: How to Bring the Sciences into Democracy*, Cambridge, MA: Harvard University Press.

—— and Callon, Michel (1981) 'Unscrewing the Big Leviathan: How Actors Macrostructure Reality', in K. Knorr and A. Cicourel (eds), *Advances in Social Theory and Methodology: Toward an Integration of Micro and Macro Sociologies*, London: Routledge.

Levinas, Emmanuel (1969) *Totality and Infinity* (trans. A. Lingis), Pittsburgh, PA: Duquesne University Press.

—— (1985) *Ethics and Infinity: Conversations with Philippe Nemo* (trans. R. Cohen), Pittsburgh: Duquesne University Press.

—— (1987) *Time and the Other* (trans. R. Cohen), Pittsburgh, PA: Duquesne University Press.

—— (1989) 'Ethics and Politics', in S. Hand (ed.), *The Levinas Reader*, Oxford: Blackwell.

—— (1990/1933) 'The Politics of Hitlerism', *Critical Inquiry* 17(1): 62–71.

—— (1998a) 'Useless Suffering', in *Entre Nous: On Thinking of the Other* (trans. M. Smith and B. Harshav), New York: Columbia University Press.

—— (1998b) 'Philosophy, Justice and Love', in *Entre Nous: On Thinking of the Other* (trans. M. Smith and B. Harshav), New York: Columbia University Press.

—— with Kearney, R. (1986) 'Dialogue with Emmanuel Levinas', in R. Cohen (ed.), *Face to Face with Levinas*, New York: SUNY Press.

MacKay, Fiona (2001) *Love and Politics: Women Politicians and the Ethics of Care*, London: Continuum.

Massumi, Brian (2002) 'Too Blue: Colour-Patch for an Expanded Empiricism', in *Parables for the Virtual: Movement, Affect, Sensation*, Durham, NC: Duke University Press.

Mol, Anne-Marie (2002) *The Body Multiple: Ontology in Medical Practice*, Durham, NC: Duke University Press.

Morris, Meaghan and Patton, Paul (eds) (1979) *Michel Foucault: Power, Truth, Strategy*, Sydney: Feral Publications.

Moser, Carolyn (1993) *Gender, Planning and Development*, London: Routledge.

Nancy, Jean-Luc (1991) *The Inoperative Community* (trans. P. Connor, L. Garbus, M. Holland and S. Sawhney), Minneapolis: University of Minnesota Press.

—— (1993) *The Birth To Presence* (trans. Brian Holmes et al.), Stanford, CA: Stanford University Press.

—— (2000) *Being-Singular-Plural*, Stanford, CA: Stanford University Press.

—— (2005) Conference paper presented at 'Adieu Derrida' seminar series, Birkbeck College, London, May.

Nealon, Jeffrey T. (1998) *Alterity Politics: Ethics and Performative Subjectivity*, Durham, NC: Duke University Press.

Nietzsche, F. (1954) 'Thus Spake Zarathustra', in W. Kaufmann (ed.), *The Portable Nietzsche*, New York: Vintage.

—— (1967/1887) 'On the Genealogy of Morals', in *On the Genealogy of Morals and Ecco Homo* (trans. W. Kaufmann), New York: Vintage.

—— (1967/1887) 'Ecce Homo', in *On the Genealogy of Morals and Ecco Homo* (trans. W. Kaufmann), New York: Vintage.

—— (1982) *Daybreak* (trans. R. Hollingdale), Cambridge: Cambridge University Press.

Noddings, Nel (1984) *Caring*, Berkeley and Los Angeles: University of California Press.

Nussbaum, Martha (1986) *The Fragility of Goodness: Luck and Ethics in Greek Tragedy and Philosophy*, Cambridge: Cambridge University Press.

—— (1999) 'The Professor of Parody', *The New Republic*, 22 February (Available at http: www.tnr.com/archive).

Oliver, Kelly (2001) *Witnessing: Beyond Recognition*, Minneapolis: University of Minnesota Press.

Olsen, Gary A. (2002) 'The Contemporary Sophist: An Interview with Stanley Fish', *Justifying Belief: Stanley Fish and the Work of Rhetoric*, New York: SUNY Press.

Patraka, V. (1999) *Spectacular Suffering: Theatre, Fascism and the Holocaust*, Bloomington: Indiana University Press.

Prigogine, Ilya (1997) *The End of Certainty: Time, Chaos and New Laws of Nature*, New York: Free Press.

—— and Stengers, Isabelle (1985) *Order Out of Chaos: Man's New Dialogue with Nature*, Flamingo: London.

Rabinow, Paul (ed.) (1997) *Michel Foucault: Ethics, Subjectivity and Truth, Essential Works of Michel Foucault*, Volume 1 (trans. Robert Hurley et al.), New York: The New Press.

Radstone, Susannah (2001) 'Social Bonds and Psychical Order: Testimonies', *Cultural Values* 5(1): 59–78.

Ranciere, Jacques (1999) *Disagreement: Politics and Philosophy*, Minneapolis: University of Minnesota Press.

Riley, D. (2000) *Words of Selves*, Stanford, CA: Stanford University Press.

Rose, Nikolas (2000) *Powers of Freedom*, Cambridge: Cambridge University Press.

Rosengarten, M. (2004) 'The Challenge of HIV for Feminist Theory', *Feminist Theory*, Special Issue: Feminist Theory and/of Science (Guest Editor: Susan M. Squier) 5(2): 205–22.

Ruddick, Sara (1989) *Maternal Thinking*, New York: Ballantine Books.

Shabi, Rachel (2006) 'Making Human Drama out of a Political Crisis', *The Guardian*, Media Section, 9 January, p. 3.

Shapiro, Michael (2004) 'Radicalising Democratic Theory: Social Space in Connolly, Deleuze and Ranciere', Conference Paper, Jacques Ranciere Conference, Goldsmiths College.

Silverman, Kaja (1996) *Threshold of the Visible World*, London: Routledge.

Smart, B. (1998) 'Foucault, Levinas and the Subject of Responsibility', in J. Moss (ed.), *The Later Foucault*, London: Sage.

Smith, John and Jenks, Chris (2005) 'Complexity, Ecology and the Materiality of Information', *Theory, Culture & Society*, Special Issue on Complexity 22(5): 141–64.

Sontag, Susan (2003) *Regarding the Pain of Others* London: Penguin.

Spelman, Elizabeth V. (1991) 'Feeling Virtuous and the Virtue of Feeling', in C. Card, *Feminist Ethics* Lawrence, Kansas: University Press of Kansas.

Spivak, Gayatri (1988) 'Can the Subaltern Speak?', in C. Nelson and L. Grossberg (eds), *Marxism and the Interpretation of Culture*, Urbana: University of Illinois Press.

—— (1993) *The PostColonial Critic*, New York: Routledge.

—— (1998) 'Cultural Talks in the Hot Peace: Revisiting the "Global Village"', in P. Cheah and B. Robbins (eds), *Cosmopolitics: Thinking and Feeling Beyond the Nation*, Minneapolis: University of Minnesota Press.

Stengers, Isabelle (2000) *The Invention of Modern Science*, Minneapolis: University of Minnesota Press.

—— (2001) 'Whitehead and the Laws of Nature', paper presented at Goldsmiths College, University of London.

—— (2002) 'Beyond Conversation: the Risks of Peace', in Catherine Keller and Anne Daniell (eds), *Process and Difference: Between Cosmological and Post-structuralist Postmodernisms*, New York: State University of New York Press.

—— (2005) 'The Cosmopolitical Proposal', in Bruno Latour and Peter Weibel (eds), *Making Things Public: Atmospheres of Democracy*, Cambridge, MA: MIT Press.

Strathern, Marilyn (1996) 'Cutting the Network', *Journal of the Royal Anthropological Institute* 2(3): 517–35.

—— (2002) 'Externalities in Comparative Guise', *Economy & Society* 31(2): 250–67.

Stringer, Rebecca (2003) *Knowing Victims: Feminism, Ressentiment and the Category 'Victim'*, Unpublished doctoral thesis, Australian National University.

Toronto, Joan (2000) 'Time's Place', Unpublished conference paper presented at Gendering Ethics Conference, University of Leeds.

Urry, John (2005) 'The Complexities of the Global', *Theory, Culture & Society* 22(5): 235–54.

—— and Law, J. (2004) 'Enacting the Social', *Economy & Society* 33(3): 390–410.

Villa, Dana (1996) *Arendt and Heidegger: The Fate of the Political*, Princeton: Princeton University Press.

—— (1999) Politics, Philosophy, Terror: Essays on the Thought of Hannah Arendt, Princeton: Princeton University Press.

Walker, Margaret Urban (1998) *Moral Understandings: A Feminist Study in Ethics*, New York: Routledge.

Warren, Karen J. (1990) 'The Power and Promise of Ecological Feminism', *Environmental Ethics* 12(2): 125–46.

Warren, Ralph (1966) *Who Speaks for the Negro?*, Vintage Books: New York.

Whitehead, Alfred N. (1985)(1978/1929) *Process and Reality: An Essay in Cosmology*, New York: The Free Press.

—— (1985/1926) *Science and the Modern World*, London: Free Association Books.

Williams, Patricia (1991) *The Alchemy of Race and Rights: Diary of a Law Professor*, Cambridge, MA: Harvard University Press.

Young, Iris Marion (1996) 'Communication and the Other: Beyond Deliberative Democracy', in Seyla Benhabib (ed.), *Democracy and Difference: Contesting the Boundaries of the Political*, Princeton: Princeton University Press.

Young-Bruehl, Elizabeth (1982) *Hannah Arendt: For Love of the World*, New Haven, CT: Yale University Press.

Ziarek, Ewa (2001) *An Ethics of Dissensus: Postmodernity, Feminism and the Politics of Radical Democracy*, Stanford, CA: Stanford University Press.

Index